Grieving God's Way

Grieving God's Way

Margaret Brownley
Haiku by Diantha Ain

WINEPRESS WP PUBLISHING

Praises for Grieving God's Way

Margaret Brownley, with great insight and compassion, fashions ordinary words into loving images that penetrate into the deepest regions of the heart to soften our pain and give us hope.

—Loya M. Coffin,
Editor of Bereavement Magazine

Through Margaret Brownley's talented insights, daily occurrences take on new perspectives, softening grief's pain, and turning hearts in new directions.

—Andrea Gambill
Helped to organize the first
National Board of Directors for *The Compassionate Friends.*

Margaret Brownley offers those who grieve sympathetic support informed by hard-won insights into the timeless truths found in God's Word. Margaret has gone through the valley of the shadow and emerged with a message of comfort and hope. This is a book not just for people of faith, but for those who are questioning, disillusioned or otherwise authentically seeking the comfort and help of God. I cannot think of a more helpful book for those who grieve.

—Pastor Jeff Cheadle
Simi Valley Presbyterian Church

Why just *go* through your grief when you can *grow* through your grief by using the helpful guidelines Margaret Brownley presents in *Grieving God's Way?* Margaret's insightful writing and Diantha Ain's inspiring Haiku point the way through grief to new life. As a woman who has experienced the grief of losing a husband and three children in a plane crash, I can say a loud *Amen* to all that is written in this book.

—Diane Bringgold Brown
Author

Margaret Brownley and Diantha Ain are two multi-talented women who understand the heaviness of grief, having each lost a child. They also understand the healing power of friendship, faith, love, and just "being there". If you or someone you know has suffered a recent loss, or is still hurting from a past loss, I highly recommend this book. I'm a longtime fan of both of these writers. Their caring hearts, together with their gift of words, will make the journey to healing a little easier for grieving souls.

—Martha Bolton
Staff writer for Bob Hope and
author of more than 50 books

WinePress Publishing, PO Box 428, Enumclaw, WA 98022. The views expressed or implied in this work do not necessarily reflect those of WinePress Publishing. The author is ultimately responsible for the design, content and editorial accuracy of this work.

Unless otherwise noted, all Scriptures are taken from the Holy Bible, New International Version, Copyright © 1973, 1978, 1984 by the International Bible Society. Used by permission of Zondervan Publishing House. The "NIV" and "New International Version" trademarks are registered in the United States Patent and Trademark Office by International Bible Society.

ISBN 1-57921-664-1
Library of Congress Catalog Card Number: 2003104806

It takes a village to write a book, and I would like to thank the many wonderful people in my life who made this book possible. My thanks go to Michael Larsen and Elizabeth Pomada, friends and literary agents, who never lost faith in the book; to Diantha Ain for her touching haiku and friendship; to Lee Duran for her encouragement and ability to make me laugh in the darkest of times; to Pastor Jeff Cheadle of the Simi Valley Presbyterian Church for inspiration and wisdom; to my husband, George, for his undying love and support; to all of the wonderful people at *Bereavement* magazine for their dedication in helping the bereaved and for thinking that I had something to offer.

Finally, I wish to thank those of you who told me to "get over it" because you inspired me to seek and to find another way—God's way.

When grieving God's way,
our faith becomes a beacon
that guides our footsteps.
                                    —Diantha Ain

For Kevin
in loving memory

Contents

". . . Listen closely to my words . . . for they are life to those who find them and health to a man's whole body."

(Proverbs 4:2–22)

PART ONE

Healing the Grieving Body

Society's Way:
Numb rather than heal the pain

God's Way:
Healing through healthy choices

Introduction to Part 1

Toning my muscles
energizes my psyche,
which comforts my soul.

When a loved one dies, the body reacts with shock. The circulation slows; we feel cold and disoriented. Breathing is shallow. After the numbness wears off, bones ache and muscles are sore. Food holds no interest, and although we might fall exhausted into bed each night, we often can't sleep—or we sleep too much. This is how the body grieves.

Many people neglect to take care of themselves following the loss of a loved one. Worse, some people try to deaden the pain with alcohol or drugs. Studies show that neglecting health during bereavement puts us at a higher risk for cancer, depression, and heart disease. Substance abuse prevents healing altogether.

Grieving God's way requires us to trust that God will lead us through the darkness, heal our pain, and bring peace to our weary soul.

1

BREATHING LESSONS

When lungs are stricken
by overpowering grief,
each breath drowns in tears.

Take a deep breath.

If you're grieving a loved one, chances are you haven't taken a deep breath for quite some time. The physical and emotional stress of grief can do an enormous amount of harm to the mind and body. We become so caught up in our pain that we literally forget to breathe.

In both Greek and Hebrew, the word for breath also means spirit. Studies have shown that deep, slow breathing can strengthen the heart, tone muscles, slow the effects of aging, increase energy, improve digestion, and alleviate certain emotional problems. It can even help us lose weight by improving metabolism.

Shallow breathing, the kind that is so prevalent during grief, fills only the upper parts of our bodies with air. It never occurs to us that the headaches, back pain, indigestion, or depression that plagues us during the darkest days of grief might be caused by our bodies simply crying out for oxygen.

Take a deep breath. Take a lot of deep breaths. Stand tall and concentrate on the center of energy just above your navel where each breath should begin and end. Stretch your diaphragm by filling your stomach with air, and you'll feel the tension fade away and a surge of new energy take its place.

In her delightful book *A Natural History of the Senses*, Diane Ackerman writes, "At this moment you are breathing some of the same molecules once breathed by Leonardo da Vinci, William Shakespeare, Anne Bradstreet, or Colette. Inhale deeply. Think of 'The Tempest.' Air works the bellows of our lungs, and it powers our cells."

Take another deep breath; absorb all of God's creation, and breathe in a little bit of Shakespeare. It is good for not only the body but also the soul.

"In His hand is the life of every creature and the breath of all mankind."
(Job 12:10)

2

WITH OPEN HANDS

*The laying of hands
miraculously eases
the pain of grieving.*

Have you looked at your hands lately? What do they say about you and your state of mind? What do they reveal about your soul?

Hands mirror our emotions. No secret is safe. One glance at our hands, and even strangers know if we're nervous or angry, outgoing or shy.

We hold our hands open in friendship and clap them together in excitement or joy. We open our hands when bearing gifts and close them when we feel discouraged, disheartened, or even lonely.

A young mother receives her newborn child with open hands; a new bride spreads her fingers to show off her new ring. A baseball player hits a homerun and is greeted by teammates with a "high-five." We say goodbye by waving, palm outward, as if trying to stay connected to a departing friend or family member for as long as possible.

We wring our hands in despair and confusion. When we grieve, we ball our hands on our laps or clutch them to our chest. Mourners at a funeral hold their hands very differently than do guests at a wedding. In sign language, the sign for grief is two closed hands palm to palm, twisting next to the heart.

In Henri Nouwen's inspiring book on prayer, *With Open Hands*, he urges us to release our tightly clenched fists and open our hearts to God.

Hold your hands open as if you were bearing gifts. Lift your open hands in prayer, and reach outward to hug a friend, pet an animal, or encourage a child. Lay an open palm on a photo of your loved one, and let all of the love that you feel for that person pour through your fingertips. Instead of striking out in anger, reach out in compassion, love, and understanding.

When we close our hands, we close our hearts. You can't open one without opening the other.

"Then he put his hands on her, and immediately she straightened up and praised God."

(Luke 13:13)

3

A Room of Her Own

In the gazebo,
I do my woolgathering
with warm memories.

Virginia Wolff understood the importance of having a place of her own. So did Chris Madden, who wrote in her book *A Room Of Her Own: Women's Personal Spaces*, "I firmly believe that to give back to our relationships, careers, families, and passions, we must pull in for short moments to take care of ourselves, and then we can return to our lives, renewed, refreshed, and ready to continue the drama of our days with all the joys, sorrows, pleasures, and stresses that go with it."

Grief is tough and demanding; it depletes us until we seem to have nothing left to give. If you haven't taken time for yourself since the death of your loved one, plan some "short moments" alone.

One mother carves out fifteen-minute segments in her busy day for meditation and prayer by setting a timer. Her four-and five-year-olds know not to disturb her until the timer goes off.

A pastor friend burns a candle when she needs quiet time away from the family to work on her sermons. The family knows not to disturb her when the candle is lit.

Jesus often went to a garden or climbed a mountain to spend quiet time with God.

Renew yourself by setting your alarm a few minutes earlier and spending quiet time alone before the rest of the family rises. Take a refreshing break during lunch or by simply turning off the TV. Pull back for a while by not answering the phone or by hiring someone to do your errands.

Renew, refresh, pull back. The moments might be short, but they can add up to a very long and satisfying life.

"It is good to wait quietly for the salvation of the LORD."
(Lamentations 3:26)

Healing Ways

Prayer is essential to our physical and emotional health. It lowers blood pressure and helps relieve stress. Prayer forces us to put our thoughts in order, our feelings into words. Prayer helps us to focus on something other than our inner pain; it reminds us that someone else is in charge.

4

WRITING IT ALL DOWN

Love letters to you
are carefully encoded
within my journal.

Writing is a lost art. Letter and diary writing was a way of life for our ancestors. The quick messages sent by e-mail can't replace the emotional cleansing that comes with writing a long letter or pouring heart and soul onto the pages of a diary.

Approximately half of the New Testament is made up of letters. Our ancestors wrote during times of stress or change, bringing diaries to America on the *Mayflower* and taking them with them during the great migration west. When these early pioneers were away from home and loved ones, diaries helped them make sense of a brave new world and face the many changes ahead.

Letters written during war did more than keep families in touch; they helped soldiers and their loved ones cope by providing outlets for fear and loneliness. Historians record events, but the soul of a nation is recorded in its letters and diaries.

Today, some people keep grief diaries or write long letters to the deceased. My daughter wrote a letter to her brother and burned it on his grave. The pages fanned open like loving hands, releasing her pain and turning her anger to ashes.

In *The Artist's Way,* Julie Cameron tells us to drain the brain by writing morning pages. "Morning pages are three pages of long-hand writing, strictly stream-of-consciousness. . . . Although occasionally colorful, the morning pages are often negative, frequently fragmented, often self-pitying, repetitive, stilted, babyish, angry or bland—even silly sounding. Good!"

Write a letter. Write morning or *mourning* pages. Start a diary. It doesn't matter which you choose—as long as you write. If you can't think of anything to say, then finish one of these sentences:

- I'm angry because . . .
- I'm so lonely when . . .
- I wish . . .
- I miss . . .
- I want . . .
- I can't stand . . .
- God help me to . . .
  Write it down. It's good for the health.

"This is what the LORD . . . says: 'Write in a book all the words I have spoken to you.'"

(Jeremiah 30:2)

We can measure our healing by looking back through the pages of our grief.

5

TEDDY BEARS AND OTHER WARM FUZZIES

*Teddy bears give me
the same warm, fuzzy feeling
thoughts of you convey.*

Whenever Nancy feels lonely, she buries her nose in her late husband's flannel shirt, and his scent brings back happy memories.

Lisa finds her warm fuzzies in her church's grief group. "After our meeting, everyone hugs. I carry the warm feelings around for days."

Warm fuzzies make us feel good—sometimes *too* good. We all seek out people who support our views and make us feel loved and secure. But what if we're doing something that's not good for us? What we need at such times is honesty, not warm fuzzies.

Grief absorbs our attention, narrows our scope, and distorts and disguises our feelings, making us lose perspective. Sometimes it takes a friend to recognize morbid grief, clinical depression, or chemical dependency. Sometimes it takes a friend to point us in the right direction.

Former First Lady Betty Ford has been very candid about her own chemical dependency and how her family convinced her she needed help.

Separating the unrealistic expectations of family and friends from genuine concern can be a challenge. Most of us are irritated when someone makes some thoughtless remark, such as, "Aren't you over it yet?" Most of the time, our irritation is justified; grieving God's way takes longer than most people realize. But concerns voiced by family or friends about alcohol, drug use, or depression cannot and *must* not be dismissed.

Warm fuzzies are great and can help us through difficult times. More serious problems require more serious action. If a family member voices concern, listen.

God talks to us in many ways, sometimes even through our friends. If two or more people mention the same problem, seek professional help.

"The Spirit helps us in our weakness."

(Romans 8:26)

6

STAND UP AND HEAL

Possibilities
supercede life's tragedies
when we grieve God's way.

Whenever I'm about to give a speech, my husband always reminds me of the three S words—*stand*, *speak*, and *sit*.

When we stand before an audience, we signal authority and power. Our words carry more weight.

Experts know that standing improves thinking skills. The very act itself allows the lungs to work better and the blood to flow more efficiently to the brain.

Standing also has a spiritual significance. In almost every biblical text describing the healing powers of Jesus, the person healed either stood or was told to stand.

> *"He placed his hands on her, and right away, she stood up straight and praised God"*
>
> *(Luke 13:13).*

> *"All of a sudden a man with swollen legs stood up in front of him"*
> *(Luke 14:2).*

"Then Jesus told the man, 'You may get up and go. Your faith has made you well'"

(Luke 17:19).

"[T]he boy looked dead and almost everyone said he was. But Jesus took hold of his hand and made him stand up"

(Mark 9:26–27).

Everything we do of any real importance requires us to stand, from getting married to being sworn in as president. Standing signals readiness. In the Bible, believers often stood to show faith. Crowds stand in the bleachers to cheer on a team. We stand in church to sing our praises to God. We stand to show respect for man and country.

We stand in joy; we stand in respect and awe. We stand divided or together. We stand in love and faith, conviction and passion.

And, as the Bible repeatedly tells us, we must also stand to heal—if only in spirit.

"He makes my feet like the feet of a deer; he enables me to stand on the heights."

(2 Samuel 22:34)

7

Is Anyone Listening?

When I watch goldfish
swimming around serenely,
my soul swims with them.

It's been said that God gave us two ears and one mouth because He wants us to listen twice as much as we talk. We might all be healthier if we followed that advice.

In her book *Walking On Water*, Madeleine L'Engle tells us that listening also helps in creativity: "Shakespeare knew how to listen to his work, and so he often wrote better than he could write; Bach composed more deeply, more truly than he knew; Rembrandt's brush put more of the human spirit on canvas than Rembrandt could comprehend."

Instead of listening to our world, we stare at blank walls or still photos. Rather than focusing on others, we think only of our loss. Instead of listening to God, we let our sobs drown out His words.

Those of us in grief could learn a lesson from the Masters.

"Listen, O heavens, and I will speak; hear, O earth, the words of my mouth."

(Deuteronomy 32:1)

Listen to your body

What are the aches and pains telling you about your health or state of mind? Are they telling you that you're eating or sleeping too much or too little? Not getting enough exercise or sunlight? Depending too much on alcohol or drugs? Neglecting the basics of good nutrition?

Listen to your environment

When was the last time you heard laughter or music? Listen to your friends and family. If you listen hard enough, you'll know that they're grieving losses, too—and one of those losses could be the failure to engage your attention.

Listen to God

God teaches us to listen to His word by talking to us in many different ways. Sometimes He talks to us through prayers and dreams. Sometimes He talks to us through others. Be still and listen for His message.

Listen to the world around you

And you'll live better than you know how to live.

Listen to those you care about

And you'll love deeper than you know how to love.

"Pay attention . . . and listen to me; be silent, and I will speak."
(Job 33:31)

8

WALKING THROUGH GRIEF

A brisk morning walk
along a familiar route
eases my sorrow.

Want to know what to give someone who is depressed, has low self-esteem, or lacks confidence and motivation? Walking shoes.

Researchers at Harvard Medical School found that a regular walking program increases confidence, self-esteem, and motivation. It lifts the spirits, restores a sense of control, and helps build inner strength.

If you're feeling depressed, lonely, or tired, take a walk.

Walk around the block, through a park, or to the shopping mall. If walking is difficult for you physically, walk a short distance—the length of one house or one car, perhaps—for starters. Following hip replacement surgery, a ninety-year-old relative proudly boasted that she walked "the length of four rose bushes."

Walk briskly or walk slowly, but always walk with passion. Center yourself as you walk. Look upward. Say a prayer of thanksgiving. Let each step be a celebration of God's many blessings.

Walk in the morning mist, the evening glow, or the mid-day brilliance. You'll sleep better, eat better, and, more than anything else, grieve better.

"*By his light I walked through darkness!*"

(Job 20:3)

9

THE HEALING SUN

*Basking in the sun
can melt away one layer
of grief's icy coat.*

The sun has gotten a bum rap in recent years. It has been blamed for everything from wrinkles to skin cancer, but in our zeal to remain healthy and young, we've forgotten one very important thing: without the sun, life as we know it would cease to exist.

The sun is essential for strong bones. Ultraviolet light changes certain cholesterol in your skin to vitamin D. Without this important vitamin, the body is unable to absorb calcium.

The lack of sunlight affects us in other ways: more than eleven million people in the United States suffer Seasonal Affective Disorder (SAD), and a far greater number experience the "winter blues." The lack of sunlight can bring on depression, weight gain, and even thoughts of suicide. A little bit of sunlight has been shown to improve job performance and schoolchildren's test scores.

People who have a seasonal disorder get a double whammy when the grief journey takes them through the winter months.

Although you might feel like hibernating in a cave somewhere, you'll feel a whole lot better by walking in the sun. If you're afraid of ultraviolet rays, walk in the early morning hours—or the late afternoon. No one knows how much sunlight we need for optimum health and mood enhancement, but many doctors recommend at least ten minutes a day.

Clean your windows until they sparkle, and open your curtains wide. Hang your sheets outside to dry, and take a little sunlight to bed with you. Let the sun shine on your grief, and feel the heavy sadness melt away.

> *"But for you who revere my name, the sun of righteousness will rise with healing in its wings."*
>
> *(Malachi 4:2)*

10

THE SWEET GIFT OF MEMORY

Once the grieving stops,
the soul can begin to laugh
at sweet memories.

As we grow older, we become ever mindful of the thing we call memory. We answer an obscure question on a TV quiz show without effort but can't find our keys. We know the statistics of a favorite baseball player but draw a blank at an important meeting.

Memory can be capricious and unpredictable; it can embarrass and confound; it can do us proud. Memory gives us the power to travel back in time, to come face to face again with people in our past, to bridge the past with the future. To remember a loved one.

But what if we forget? What if we lose all memory of the one we lost? This is a question that haunts many of us as we grow older. It haunted an elderly relative of mine who recently complained that she could no longer recall the face of her long dead husband.

Recent research is encouraging. Studies show that memory can be affected by disease, alcohol, drugs, or trauma, but memory loss is not an inevitable part of aging. Memories can last a lifetime. Eva Hart, only seven years old when she and her parents traveled on the *Titanic*, recalled every detail of the sinking ship that claimed her father until her own death eighty-four years later.

Keeping our brains healthy and, therefore, our memories intact should be part of every health program. Dieting and stress can poke holes in anyone's memory bank, and so can depression. Exercise, good nutrition, and sleep are important, especially as we age.

Reading, doing crossword puzzles, studying the Bible, learning to play a musical instrument, and socializing all have a positive impact on the memory. Sometimes we forget simply because we don't pay attention.

Our loved one lives in our memory, so that memory is worth protecting. Cherish the memories that you have, and preserve the ones you are creating. Memories are among the most precious gifts we have; if we take care of them, they'll be among the most lasting gifts.

"A righteous man will be remembered forever."

(Psalm 112:6)

11

GRIEF IS NOT AN ILLNESS

When you have good days,
take time to reward yourself
for good behavior.

When my friend Mary signed up to run a marathon, her family expressed concern because she had cancer. Running was for the healthy. "I *am* healthy," my friend insisted. "I'm a healthy person who just happens to have cancer."

Grief is not an illness, but some people treat it as such. The loss of a loved one is all too often an excuse for giving up on God and losing hope.

In her book *Anatomy of the Spirit*, Caroline Myss, Ph.D., tells us, "The process of curing is passive." She goes on to explain how we tend to give ourselves over to a doctor or prescribed treatment rather than actively challenging the illness ourselves. "Healing, on the other hand, is an active and internal process," she writes, "that includes investigating one's attitudes, memories, and beliefs with the desire to release all negative patterns that prevent one's full emotional and spiritual recovery."

There's no cure for grief, but there is healing for those who refuse to give into depression and despair. Confront the painful memories, and let go of the negatives. Start acting and thinking like a healthy person who happens to be grieving.

Mary died of cancer the day after she returned from an African safari. She was healthy to the end.

"O LORD my God, I called to you for help and you healed me."

(Psalm 30:2)

Healing Ways

"Jesus said, 'Take care of my sheep'"

(John 21:16).

Become a Caregiver. Having to care for something or someone gives life purpose and meaning and focuses our attention outward. Some people who live alone find it comforting to take care of a pet or even a garden. Look around. Chances are that everyone you meet could use a little loving care.

12

GOD'S WAY

As time marches on,
we can best get back in step
by grieving God's way.

Almost every dieter hits a brick wall. Days or even weeks go by without any noticeable loss of weight. It's enough to make you want to sink your teeth into the nearest candy bar.

Those of us in grief hit the same kind of wall. We reach a point where we seem to be stuck in depression, and it looks as if things are never going to improve. Whether we call this a brick wall or a plateau, it's God's way.

Mountains don't grow gradually; they grow in spurts. A mountain range can rise as much as twenty feet or more during an earthquake. Then all is quiet—or so it seems. But miles beneath the ground, the earth must adjust to the new landscape, and this adjusting can take years.

Scientists once thought that the human body grew gradually, but, as any parent knows, children grow in spurts and, yes, even "shoot up" overnight. Following a growth spurt, adolescents are often clumsy and accident prone until the brain adjusts to the body's new dimensions.

The grief plateau or the dieter's wall serves a useful purpose in that this slowing down allows the body to adjust to the many physical and emotional changes that are taking place. Whether a person shoots up a foot, loses ten pounds, or is traumatized by loss, the brain must make infinite adjustments to accommodate the changes.

Emotions are as taxing to the body as is physical exertion. Grief changes how a person breathes, behaves, and even thinks, and this change is reflected in speech, movement, and outlook. The brain can't possibly process this all at once, so we shut down. We become more reclusive to prevent outside stimuli from interfering with the work of the brain. Depression keeps us from taking on more than we can handle. It feels as though we are buried in a hole, but, in reality, we are in God's protective care. Once the body adjusts, we are ready to take the next step in the recovery process.

Stop and start. Stop and start. It's God's way.

"In his heart a man plans his course, but the LORD determines his steps."

(Proverbs 16:9)

Healing Ways

Celebrate the plateaus in your life. Close your eyes and imagine your body fine tuning itself to accommodate the new you. Pay attention to the areas of your life that no longer work—take care of the little things that you've neglected, put off, or avoided altogether. By creating a sense of well-being, we help body and soul prepare for the next "growth" spurt.

13

STOP AND GO

Grief is a red light
that healing turns to amber,
and wellness, to green

The shock and disbelief that come with grief serve a useful purpose. They are God's way of stopping us in our tracks. They are our body's ways of saying, "Hold on. Don't move. Something important is happening here."

Sometimes, when something's too painful to face, we override the body's system and go into overdrive. We "lose" ourselves in work. When we don't want to remember, we speed up. When we don't want to hurt, we rush around in a frenzy.

We have to keep busy, we tell ourselves, but secretly we mean to outrun this thing. But grief is a persistent stalker, dogging us every step of the way, and it always catches up with us.

In his book *Stopping: How To Be Still When You Have To Keep Going,* Dr. David Kunditz writes, "The ultimate purpose of stopping is to ensure that when we do go, we go in the direction that we want and that we are not just reacting to the pace of our lives, but choosing, moment to moment, what's best. The ultimate reason for stopping is going."

Stopping allows time for spiritual growth. Faith comes to us in quiet moments. The soul grows in stillness.

No one heals on the run. Stop. Stand still. Do nothing. Stare out of the window, gaze at the sky. Embrace the moment. Be idle for a moment, an hour, or a day. Consider going on a retreat or vacation. Play hooky from work. Stop, so you can go.

"Stop and consider God's wonders."

(Job 37:14)

Healing Ways

Journal. *It is written* is a phrase used more than ninety times in the Bible. It was God's way of saying, "This is important." Writing out our pain helps us sort through feelings and put things in perspective. It's a way of saying, "I'm hurting, and this is important."

14

CHARGE NOW: PAY LATER

When grieving God's way,
blessed dividends reward
all those who invest.

B uy now, pay later, blazes an ad in the Sunday newspaper. "No payment due until after Christmas," reads a sign in front of an appliance shop. Paying with a credit card or install-ment plan is the American way of life.

Some people live as if they have an emotional credit card. They lose a loved one and, instead of dealing with the loss, ignore it, pretend that it didn't happen, or relegate it to the future.

The problem is that postponed grief compounds interest at an alarming rate. Depression, substance abuse, stress, and health prob-lems are just some of the penalties endured when we fail to grieve God's way, and try, instead, to postpone grief or ignore it altogether.

Make a list of all your past losses, and determine whether each was adequately grieved. Remember, no loss is too small to grieve. A list might include losing out on a promotion, breaking up with someone, losing a pet, striking out during a Little League game, or failing to go after a dream.

You might even discover "hidden" anniversaries that affect you emotionally. One woman was surprised to discover that her annual depression corresponded with the month that her father walked out on the family. Once she took the time to work through the anger and grieve her loss, the depression went away.

For the greatest emotional security and peace of mind, ensure that all grief is paid in full.

"Let no debt remain outstanding, except the continuing debt to love one another . . ."

(Romans: 13:8)

15

HEALING THROUGH TRAVEL

Adventuring forth
to meet new people helps me
leave my loss behind.

Jill Hill commemorated the tenth anniversary of her daughter's death with a 1000-km bicycle ride across Ontario. Her journey, called "Miles of Memories," allowed her to stay connected to her daughter in a way that symbolized her own personal journey of grief and recovery.

One grieving widow regained self-confidence by hiking up a mountain. "I figured if I could make it up a mountain, I could survive anything."

Traveling teaches us a lot about our own inner strengths and capabilities. Travel takes us away from our normal roles and frees us to try new things, to meet new challenges, to redefine who we are and what we want out of life.

Carol Rivendell, cofounder of Wild Women Adventures in Northern California, was quoted in the Los Angeles Times: "When there's new music to dance to, you immediately start doing new steps."

Travel helps us gain a whole new perspective on life. You can be active or simply lay on the beach. You can go whitewater rafting or shop for antiques.

In Luke 22:25, Jesus cautioned His disciples to travel light. This is God's way of telling us to leave our burdens at home.

As a traveler, you are no longer defined by your grief; you are now an active adventurer, very much involved in life.

So pack your bags, but travel light—and don't forget your "dancing" shoes.

"Jesus traveled about from one town and village to another, proclaiming the good news of the kingdom of God."

(Luke 8:1)

For your journey through the desert of grief

The key to any successful trip is good planning, but not every trip or journey is eagerly anticipated, and some trips are harder to plan than others. Grief is a journey of the heart and soul that often comes when we least expect it, and it almost always takes us where we don't want to go. We muddle our way through grief like a traveler with no map, no luggage, and no credit cards. It's a journey filled with reluctant travelers.

Wherever you are in your grief, you can count on more tough times ahead. There is no one-way ticket for the pain that comes with loss, but a little planning will help you better face the emotional delays, setbacks, and derailments that every grief traveler must face.

Fix up a "travel" corner in your favorite room, perhaps in front of the fireplace or by your favorite chair. Gather the things you need for your journey, and plan to update weekly as needed. Following is a list of staples to get you started:

- A Bible
- A comforter and a pillow
- A teddy bear or other stuffed animal
- A box of tissues
- Bubble bath
- A photo album
- A good book to read
- A fresh rose or orchid
- A bright-colored balloon
- Something delicious to eat (chocolates)
- Hand or body lotion in your favorite scent
- Candles
- Blank notepads for writing down thoughts and memories
- A new pen that is used only to record your journey
- Telephone numbers of your support group
- Herbal tea and a china teapot
- Videos—preferably funny or light-hearted movies
- CDs—music that lifts your spirits
- Firewood
- Something that symbolizes love to you—
- Something to hold close to your heart.

"Not fare well, but fare forward, voyagers."

(T.S. Eliot)

The Lord had said to Abram, "Leave your country, your people and your father's household and go to the land I will show you."
(Genesis 12:1)

16

HEALING THROUGH PLAY

Your favorite games
stare down at me from their shelf,
daring me to play.

Few animals play as adults, but humans do. Humans play at all ages. Not only is play a great way to restore energy, optimism, and hope but also research shows that play actually helps in mate selection. Playful women seem more youthful and therefore more appealing to men; women regard playful men as safe.

Play puts us back in control. We get to choose how to hit the ball or play the game and for how long.

Play offers other advantages. Have you ever noticed that playful people seem to have an easier time getting through grief than those who are content to follow more serious pursuits?

In *Childhood and Society,* Erik Erikson described play as "the most natural, self-healing measure" that life can offer. So put aside some healing time each day to play.

In a *Psychology Today* article, Hara Estroff Marano wrote. "At the beach we are all children." So take a trip to the beach and play as a child. Run into the waves; build a castle. Play volleyball.

Play hopscotch with a child. Fly a kite. Ride a carousel. Buy an ice cream cone. Blow bubbles. Plan a family outing at the county fair. Go horseback riding. Swing in the moonlight. Dance in the sun.

Pray with childlike faith.

"Unless you change and become like little children, you will never enter the kingdom of heaven."

(Matthew 18:3)

God is the best medicine for grief-related depression, and there are no worrisome side effects.

17

IT REALLY IS IN YOUR HEAD

Losing a loved one
can turn a stouthearted soul
to Humpty Dumpty.

Six months after my son died, I walked into my bedroom and suddenly couldn't breathe. I was rushed to ER and placed on oxygen. The memory of my son's last days in the hospital hit me full force, and my symptoms increased.

Not one doctor who treated me that day thought to ask me what had happened in recent months that could have caused such stress, and therein lies one of the major problems of modern health care. Often, a doctor will treat a headache, unaware that grief counseling, not medication, is needed.

But it's not just doctors who are to blame; we have to accept some of the responsibility ourselves. Those of us who were taught that penicillin was a miracle drug or that a shot could cure anything grew up with little understanding of how the body heals. We seek outside cures, unaware that healing comes from within.

The job of medicine is to create an environment that makes it possible for inner healing to take place. If you break your leg, a cast will hold it in place while the bone heals. Even immunology shots depend on the immune system to ward off disease, and today, scientific research is centered on how to help the body better fight off disease by using the natural drugs in the brain, where every drug you'll ever need is said to exist.

No medicine known to mankind can cure a broken heart or a shattered soul. No shots exist that can take away your grief. But prayer and a close relationship to God can ease the suffering and heal the pain.

Healing really is all in the head.

"Set your minds on things above, not on earthly things."
(Colossians 3:2)

"Jesus Christ is the same yesterday and today and forever."
(Hebrews 13:8)

When we lose a loved one, our world changes, and nothing seems the same. How comforting to know that when our life is turned upside down, we can still count on God's continued love and constant presence.

18

"Hoppy" Meals

*A hot fudge sundae
allows my guilt freedom to
overcome my grief.*

Nothing pleases my three-year-old granddaughter more than going to her favorite fast-food restaurant and ordering what she calls a "Hoppy" meal. "A hoppy meal makes me feel good inside," she explains, and it's not hard to guess why. "Hoppy meals" come in a bright-colored box and include the latest movie character or toy.

Mealtime is anything but "hoppy" for those of us who are grieving. Nothing can dampen the appetite more than an empty chair or having to set one less place setting. So what do we do in those early weeks and months when having to eat alone only adds to our depression and grief?

Start by planning a "hoppy" meal. The menu must include your favorite foods and be served in a fun way—perhaps with candles and flowers. Set up your meal in a room other than the kitchen or dining room, if necessary. Here comes the fun part: plan a "toy" or some other special thing to go with your meal.

Following the death of his wife, Jim purchased the sound equipment that he had been wanting, and he read the manual during mealtime to keep his mind busy.

Lois reads the Bible to combat loneliness while she is dining alone. Phylis creates her healing meals by talking to her out-of-state daughter on the telephone while she eats. One woman arranges her mealtime to correspond with chat room discussions held by her Internet grief group.

Play your favorite music, watch videos, commune with nature or God. Invite a friend to dinner, a neighbor to tea, or a child to lunch. Remember, it's not a "hoppy" meal unless it makes you feel good inside.

"Man does not live on bread alone."

(Luke 4:4)

Healing Ways

Society tells us, "Get over it," as if a broken heart can be healed at will. God knows it's not that simple. He doesn't tell us, "Get over it," but He does tell us to move forward even as we weep.

"Those who sow in tears will reap with songs of joy. He who goes out weeping, carrying seed to sow, will return with songs of joy, carrying sheaves with him."

(Psalm 126: 5–6)

Heartache is love that has no where to go. By "carrying" our gifts into the world, by sharing our skills and talents with others, we allow God to use that love in wondrous ways.

19

TEA AND SYMPATHY

Your favorite blend
steeps in a cozied teapot,
wishing you could pour.

T ea is good for the body, but tea *time* is good for the soul. Tea is thought to protect against certain cancers and heart disease, but the real healing power is in the serving.

Making a pot of tea gives us a sense of purpose. It's comforting to arrange cups and saucers in an orderly way, especially when our life is in chaos. The ritual pouring of tea sets the stage for free-flowing conversation between friends or quiet meditation with God.

Invite a friend for tea and share memories of your loved one. Enjoy a cup of tea while chatting on the phone to a long-distance friend or reading God's Word. Invite a child to dress up and come to tea.

Start with a heated pot. Plan one teaspoon per person and one for the pot. Dedicate this last teaspoon to the memory of a loved one. Start with cold water and bring it to a boil. After pouring the hot water over the tea, turn the teapot gently three times—an old tradition that signifies the Holy Trinity—and let it brew for a few minutes longer. Enjoy.

"Share with God's people who are in need. Practice hospitality."
                                                    Romans 12:13

20

SURVIVING THROUGH HUMOR

If I cast a smile
when passing your photograph,
it smiles back at me.

Laughter is one of God's most healing gifts and a great coping device. Perhaps the most important thing that laughter does is help people connect to one another. Humorist Victor Borge told us, "Laughter is the shortest distance between two people."

During the last days of my son's life, he was in too much pain to communicate with words, but he managed to join in our laughter when a little dog named Mitzi came bouncing into his hospital room dressed as a nurse. For the first time in days, our spirits were elevated and we connected.

Laughter not only has helped people survive the most difficult situations known to mankind but also has tremendous healing powers. The soul and the body respond to laughter, and so does the mind. A good guffaw prevents our becoming stuck in depression and moves us through grief at a faster pace. We can't bring a loved one back, but we can change our response. By finding the humor even in tragedy, we take control and become empowered. Laughter helps us see the sunshine behind the clouds, and that is the first step toward regaining hope.

God's world is full of humor. Look hard enough and you'll find something that will tickle your funny bone. You might even hear your loved one laugh with you.

> *"A cheerful heart is good medicine, but a crushed spirit dries up the bones."*
>
> *(Proverbs 17:22)*

A Time to Laugh

It's been said that harmful humor is when people laugh *at* you; healing humor is when people laugh *with* you. Following are some of the ways that healing humor can help those in grief:

Humor heals the past. Charlie Chaplin said, "To truly laugh, you must be able to take your pain and play with it." Laughter helps us put the past in perspective. Studies show that laughing freely with others can lift morale, relieve stress, and ward off depression.

Humor touches the soul. Laughter makes us feel carefree and lighthearted and lifts our spirits. Laughter fills us with hope and gives us a sense that things will be better.

Humor is good for health. Laughter lowers blood pressure, forces deep breathing, relaxes muscles, and protects the immune system.

Humor can safeguard from burnout. Laughter makes us feel more energetic and helps us to stay positive. Laughing at ourselves restores confidence.

Humor allows us to take control. Laughter helps us see problems in a different light, and that is often the first step toward finding a solution. Humor helps us cut a problem down to size; if we can laugh about it, it can't be that bad, right?

Get Into the Humor Habit!

- Wallpaper your walls with funny cartoons.
- Buy humorous cards for yourself and stand them on your desk. They'll make not only you but also others laugh.
- Invite friends over for a BYOJ (that's "bring your own jokes") party. Give gag prizes for the funniest jokes.
- Rent your favorite comedy videos, and invite the gang over for an evening of popcorn and laughter.
- Spend time browsing the humor section of your favorite bookstore.
- Sing silly songs with a child.
- Adopt a kitten or a puppy. It's guaranteed to make you laugh.

"[A]nd a little child will lead them"

(Isaiah 11:6).

Children laugh four hundred times a day; an adult laughs only about seven to nine times a day.

Sarah said, "God has brought me laughter, and everyone who hears about this will laugh with me."

(Genesis 21:6)

21

HEALING THROUGH GRATITUDE

Joy and gratitude
make my cup runneth over,
spilling thanks to God.

The Bible tells us to give thanks for all things, but it often mentions thanksgiving in the context of sacrifice. God knows that showing gratitude is not always easy; at times, it is almost impossible.

Dr. Hans Seyre, pioneer on the study of the effect of emotions on health, was the first to suggest that gratitude was an important part of healing. Gratitude helps us recover from not only physical pain but also emotional pain. During the darkest and most anguished days of our grief, we might wonder how it is possible that the human heart—indeed, the very essence of our souls—can survive so much pain? How is it possible to feel so deeply and to love so completely that we suffer this much?

These questions can come only from the most profound gratitude. Would we want it any less? Would we really want to lose a loved one and feel nothing? Would we take the time to grieve properly or find the courage to change our lives or the strength to triumph in the face of adversity if our pain were any less?

Gratitude can be a great source of strength; appreciation of friends and family reminds us that we're not alone. Such gratitude also pays off in other ways; we naturally treat people better whom we appreciate, and this better treatment is reflected in the way they treat us. Gratitude and appreciation breed more of the same.

Gratitude is not the result of healing but the point from which all healing begins. But before we can feel gratitude, we must first open our hearts to the abundance that is ours.

Give thanks for grief's pain because it symbolizes the depth of your love. Give a gratitude offering to the charity of your choice. Find a photo of your loved one, and list the reasons you're grateful that that person was part of your life. Write a letter of gratitude to someone who least expects it. Begin every day with a sentence that begins "I'm grateful to God for . . ."

"Give thanks in all circumstances, for this is God's will for you in Christ Jesus."

(1 Thessalonians 5:18)

Healing Ways

Author Melody Beattie wrote, "Gratitude unlocks the fullness of life. It turns what we have into enough, and more."

The moment we stop counting the lonely hours and count, instead, the time spent with a loved one, we have enough.

The instant we stop focusing on loss and learn to focus, instead, on warm, loving memories, we have enough.

The moment we learn to lift our hearts in gratitude and our voices to God in praise, we have enough—and more.

22

CLAP AND HEAL

At my piano,
when I play your favorites,
I hear your applause.

Recently, my husband and I drove up the California coast, reaching Moonshadow Beach just before sunset. Much to our amazement, throngs of people stood along the side of the road watching nature's grand finale, and we pulled over to join them. A distant fog bank distorted the sun, making it seem to change shapes during its final descent. One moment the sun took on the shape of a giant hourglass; the next moment it looked like a pirate's treasure chest.

The instant the sun disappeared, the crowd applauded. I'm ashamed to say that it was the first time I had ever clapped for the sun. We clap for fireworks, actors, rock stars, and athletes. Why not clap for God's handiwork?

My little granddaughter claps for butterflies. Every time she spots one in the garden, she squeals in delight and claps her hands.

Noted playwright Oliver Hailey died while friends and family gathered around his deathbed in a standing ovation. What a wonderful tribute to a gifted man who spent a lifetime writing for the stage.

Research has proven that attending concerts and plays increases one's life span. Is it only coincidence that activities that encourage applause are beneficial to our health?

As we learn to identify and accept the many gifts that our loved ones leave behind, we gain a new appreciation for things that we once took for granted. Although we are filled with sadness and loneliness and wonder if we'll ever smile again, we also have more reasons to clap with appreciation and gratitude. One day, we'll even clap our hands in joy.

"Clap your hands, all you nations; shout to God with cries of joy."
(Psalm 47:1)

23

WHAT IT TAKES TO BE HAPPY

The gift of a smile
may cost the donor little
but has great value.

Iceland is one of the most volcanically active countries in the world. Located in the North Atlantic, Iceland's wintry nights are twenty hours long, and four thousand square miles of glaciers grace its shores. Hot, cold, isolated, and dark, it sounds like anything but paradise. Yet, according to a Gallup poll of eighteen countries taken a few years ago, Icelanders ranked as the happiest people in the world. (The United States came in fifth.)

Iceland seems to prove the contention of author and radio host Dennis Prager as expressed in his book *Happiness Is a Serious Problem:* "There is little correlation between the circumstances of people's lives and how happy they are."

Not everyone would agree. The thought of being happy again might seem impossible to a grieving widow or a childless couple enduring a third miscarriage.

Although some people naturally resist the idea, studies show that most of us will reach our normal level of happiness within a year of a major loss.

Many happy people have suffered terrible losses in their lives. Many unhappy people have not. Happy people can be rich or poor, fat or thin, smart or not-so-smart, but they all have one very important thing in common—their lives have meaning and purpose.

Sometimes, we feel as though we don't deserve happiness when a loved one dies. This idea, of course, is ridiculous. Being happy isn't selfish, nor does it take anything away from the deceased. Prager tells us that happiness is a moral obligation and that we owe it to everyone in our life to be happy.

So if you can't be happy for yourself, be happy for others. It's what God wants, and you don't even have to travel to Iceland.

"A happy heart makes the face cheerful, but heartache crushes the spirit."
(Proverbs 15:13)

Healing Ways

Don't worry, be happy! Start by fooling Mother Nature with a smile, even if you have to fake it, and you'll stimulate "feel-good" feelings in the brain. Stand up straight, shoulders back, head held high. The body will respond with renewed vitality. Kick those endorphins into high gear by taking a brisk walk. Fill your life with meaning and purpose; sign up for a Bible study class, volunteer time to your favorite charity, put your trust in the Lord, and be kind to everyone you meet!

24

SLEEP: A NECESSARY HOLIDAY

The comfort of sleep
remains elusive until
we trust God's embrace.

Someone once said that insomnia was what a person has when he lies awake all night for an hour. This definition is meant to be funny, but for those of us who have lost a loved one, insomnia is no laughing matter.

Either we can't fall asleep or we wake up too early. We spend our nights twisting and turning or watching TV. Without proper sleep, we drag around all day; we feel irritable and stressed out, and we blame it on our grief. But the truth is that we're simply exhausted. Even more worrisome, recent studies show that lack of sleep weakens the immune systems in elderly widows and widowers.

Sleep is not only beneficial for our health but also essential for our emotional well-being. According to writer Iris Murdoch, one of the benefits of sleep is that it allows us to take holidays from ourselves.

If you haven't taken a "holiday from yourself," lately, start by taking a walk. People who walk regularly fall asleep faster and stay asleep longer than those who are sedentary.

Certain scents can make you sleepy. According to a British researcher, lavender is just as effective as sleeping pills in helping elderly insomniacs fall asleep. A hot bath with honeysuckle or lavender bath salts can make you sleepy. Light jasmine candles just before bedtime, and play soft, soothing music. Treat yourself to new pillows and bedding, and lower the temperature of the room. If necessary, purchase earplugs to muffle city sounds.

Imagine yourself lying down in green pastures.

Turn your grief, your pain, and your anguish over to God. Let His love fill your soul.

Listen to the still waters.

Enjoy your "holiday."

"I will lie down and sleep in peace, for you alone, O LORD, make me dwell in safety."

(Psalm 4:8)

Healing Ways

If counting sheep doesn't put you to sleep,
try talking to the shepherd.

25

It's Not Just a Matter of Survival

One tear at a time,
my great icicle of grief
is melting away.

When my son died, the doctor gave me a prescription to numb the pain and help me sleep. I never took those pills. It wasn't because I didn't need them; the pain was so intense, at times, that I wanted to die. Sleep was out of the question. I felt tired—exhausted—shattered. I could almost feel my heart bleed, my soul die.

Still, I didn't want to numb the pain or create an artificial sleep. I didn't want to *survive* grief; I wanted to experience it. I wanted to feel it, taste it, see it, hear it, and live it. I feel the same way about grief as I feel about life.

Some people become hard and bitter following the death of a loved one. They move through life like robots, paying little or no attention to the blessings still in their lives. Afraid to open themselves up to others and afraid to love again, these people soon dry up and fade away until they're barely even a shadow of their former selves.

Don't just survive grief; live it. Let grief be a stepping-stone to a better future, a better life. Let grief be your teacher and guide, your mentor and inspiration. Let grief grow your soul, expand your heart, and nourish your spirit. Let it open the door to a deeper faith, a new commitment to life, and the source through which you reach out to others.

Grief is not survived but lived.

"He reveals the deep things of darkness, and brings deep shadows into the light."

(*Job 12:22*)

Maya Angelou wrote, "To be human is to be challenged to be more divine." Nothing makes us feel more human than grief. It strips us of our barriers. Walls that take a lifetime to build come tumbling down. Without our protective shells, we feel vulnerable, afraid, and, more than anything, human. But this is a necessary part of grief because only then can God put us back together, bit by bit, this time from the inside out.

"He heals the brokenhearted and binds up their wounds."

(*Psalm 147:3*)

26

SIGNS OF GRIEF

*Powder and paint may
hide my sadness from strangers,
but not my mirror.*

Some people lose weight following the loss of a loved one, but most of us pack on additional pounds.

We might look gaunt, tired, and lifeless and even show visible signs of aging. A friend described herself as aging a century following the death of her teenaged daughter.

Grief takes a toll emotionally, but it needn't take a toll on health or appearance. If it's been a year or more since your loss, you're probably ripe for a makeover. Throw those shoulders back and stand tall. Already you look five pounds thinner. Get a new hairdo, lose a few pounds, buy a new outfit—smile. Volunteer your time in helping others. Invest your energy in something or someone outside of your grief. Plan a vacation or a day trip. Commit yourself anew to God, and sing His praises.

Watch the recent signs of grief melt away.

"O LORD my God, I called to you for help and you healed me."
(Psalm 30:2)

27

HEALING THROUGH THE SENSES

Surveying nature,
we cannot have any doubt
that there is a God.

W e learn about the world through our senses. In her book *A Natural History of the Senses*, Diane Ackerman writes, "The senses don't just make sense of this life, they tear reality apart into vibrant morsels and reassemble them into a meaningful pattern."

Loss is felt through the senses. We miss the fragrance, the touch, the sound of a loved one. We miss the sweet taste of a loved one on our lips, the touch of their hand on ours. When we lose a loved one, it's like losing part of our sight and hearing.

Sometimes the brain is confused by the signals that the senses send, and a person feels pain when no pain exists. This explains why an arm or a leg can hurt even after it's been amputated.

Sometimes we hear or see a phantom loved one. We see a loved one in a crowd, hear a voice or laughter that is familiar, smell a loved one's fragrance, and we think that we are losing our mind, but it's only our body's sensors out of whack.

When we walk into a room full of strangers, visit an unfamiliar place, or suffer a loss, our vision and hearing are sharper, our senses of smell and touch are more keen, until we have scrutinized the new environment and our brain has deemed it safe. In times of grief, our body senses something amiss and works overtime. This takes a toll on us.

Give your overworked senses a rest. Close your eyes and listen to a symphony. Spend time in places where you wouldn't normally expect to see or hear your loved one. Look for beauty in the new patterns of your life.

"'Who touched me?' Jesus asked."

(Luke 8:45)

Healing Through Touch

A baby learns to trust its world through the sense of touch. Following the death of a love one, we revert to childlike ways. We stroke photographs and keepsakes; we run our hands over a loved one's chair and pillow, seeking to stay connected. Our fingers instinctively fall upon softness like a child looking for comfort from a mother's touch. By reaching out and touching the world around us, by reaching out to God, family, and friends, we gradually learn to trust again.

28

HOW BIRDS
LEARN TO FLY

*Sometimes compassion
offers only outstretched arms
to unburden grief.*

She's so courageous! they thought as she smiled and welcomed them to the funeral. "She's so brave!" they commented when she returned to work less than a week later. She *was* courageous, and she *was* brave—until six months later, when she fell apart.

We can probably all relate to this woman in one way or another. I know that I can. About the time everyone thought that I was—or should be—"over" it, I started to unravel. Depression hit, and I lost any desire to work. Trembling like a frightened bird, I had, in essence, lost my courage.

Anne Morrow Lindbergh addressed this problem eloquently when she wrote, "It isn't for the moment you are struck that you need courage, but for the long uphill battle to faith, sanity, and security."

Asking friends for help and support during a crisis is one thing, but how do you explain to someone who's never been in your shoes that you need their support a year or two later?

If you don't have an understanding friend, try a grief group—or, as I prefer to call them, a courage group. I grieved for two years before I attended my first meeting—it took me that long to build up enough courage. But once I got there, I felt as though I had come home. I didn't have to explain why I had unraveled; everyone at that meeting had walked in my shoes.

"Come to the edge," he said.
They said, "We are afraid."
"Come to the edge," he said.
They came.
He pushed them . . .
And they flew."

Guillaume Apollinaire, 1880–1918
French poet and philosopher

"Be kind and compassionate to one another, forgiving each other, just as Christ God forgave you."

(Ephesians 4:32)

"He has made everything
beautiful in its time."
(Ecclesiastes 3:11)

PART TWO

Healing the Grieving Soul

Society's Way:
Keep busy; don't talk or think about it.

God's Way:
Healing through beauty, art, and nature

Introduction to Part 2

Grief's turbulent tide
ebbs and flows against my soul,
eroding its shape.

We tell ourselves it can't be true; our loved one can't be dead.

We rationalize, seek answers, and bargain with God. We pretend that it's all a bad dream. The days are without form or color; the nights no longer hold the promise of dawn. Silence fills the void that was once filled with music and laughter. We are but a shadow of ourselves. This is how the soul grieves.

The soul heals when it connects to God through beauty. Beauty puts a face on God and makes His presence known. When we gaze at nature, a loved one, or a work of art, our soul immediately recognizes God and is drawn to Him.

1

Chipping Away

Tears comfort the soul
washing away our sorrow
one drop at a time.

After Michelangelo had chipped away at an eighteen-foot-high block of marble and created his famous statue of David, he was asked how he had created so much beauty from a mere block of marble. He reportedly replied that he simply chipped away everything that didn't look like David.

Grief is a marble stone that must be chipped away, little by little, day by day. With the same persistence as a sculptor, we must chip away anything that doesn't look like healing. We must chisel away the anger, scrape away the pain, and sand away the loneliness. Work hard enough, and the block eventually grows rounder and smoother and turns into a more pleasing and manageable form. New life emerges—a work of art.

What art is trapped in the stone of your grief? A more authentic self? A stronger faith? A more creative soul? A more compassionate spirit?

Sometimes it's memories that we uncover; previously forgotten moments that make us smile or move us to loving tears.

Sometimes we find another dimension of a loved one, another picture of God.

Keep chipping away, piece by piece, teardrop by teardrop. Grief can make master sculptors of us all.

"Nothing in all creation is hidden from God's sight."
                                                    (Hebrews 4:13)

2

MESSAGES FROM THE SOUL

*Communication
is the secret to success
in recovery.*

T he tension headache or twinge between the shoulders—
even that tight feeling in the middle—often sends us run
ning to the medicine chest. Instead of searching for relief,
perhaps we would do better to recognize symptoms of stress as a
message from the soul to the body telling us to *slow down, be still,
there's business to attend to, something that needs our attention, some
solution to our problem that we've not yet considered.*

If we fail to give adequate attention to our loss and recovery,
grief will express itself in ways that can affect health and well-
being. How many of us are stressed out simply because we are
grieving in society's fast, haphazard way rather than God's slow
and thoughtful way?

The problem with slowing down is that it requires time, and
few of us leave any "white space" in our days for receiving, let
alone answering, a message from our soul. We respond with amazing haste to our e-mail or telephone calls, but we generally ignore

a message that can restore our mental and physical well-being, if only we would let it.

Stress is not a disease and can, in some cases, even be a blessing. When we are stressed out during a loved one's illness, it can be a sign that we are extra alert or that we need to take a big breath and say a prayer.

The stress that comes from grief is particularly hard on us. We seem unable to concentrate, yet we're expected to make life-changing decisions. Financial realities following the death of a spouse, for example, can mean having to sell a family home or return to the work force.

Elisabeth Kubler-Ross, author of *On Death and Dying*, wrote, "Should you shield the canyons from the windstorms, you would never see the beauty of their carvings." Stress, grief, heartache, and anguish. What wonderful carvings they could make on our soul—if only we would let them.

"Be still, and know that I am God . . ."

(Psalm 46:10)

3

AVOIDING THE PAIN

Survival instincts
spontaneously kick in
when tragedy strikes.

The pain that comes with grief is excruciating, and we'll do anything to avoid it. We rationalize; we tell ourselves, *He's better off this way* or *I'm lucky that we had thirty wonderful years together.*

We intellectualize; we live in our head instead of our heart. We talk about *things* rather than *feelings*. A father copes with the loss of his murdered daughter by focusing on the legal system.

We keep busy; we work extra hours, filling every waking moment. And if that's not possible, we allow ourselves to become passively distracted by TV or movies. Sometimes we seek solace through alcohol, drugs, or food.

We avoid grief by spending too much money or turning to sex. We run, we hide, we ignore, and we erase, and all these things work—for awhile. All these things bring short-term relief. But the day will come when we can run no more.

Make a list of all of the things you do to avoid grief. List all of the places and people you avoid, the tasks you put off, and the business that remains unfinished.

Move grief out of your head and into your heart. Move grief away from things and back to feelings. Move grief away from busyness and into solitude. Move grief into God's hands.

"It is better to take refuge in the LORD than to trust in man."
(Psalm 118:8)

4

SETTING THE STAGE FOR HEALING

On dark, cloudy days
thoughts of our time together
create a rainbow.

When starting to write a new novel, I first set the stage by hanging pictures of my characters and setting on my office walls. If the story is set in nineteenth-century Kansas, for example, I'll scour magazines until I find the appropriate pictures. Sometimes paper dolls and old postcards help me capture the tone and spirit of the times.

Quite by accident, I discovered that what helps the creative process is also helpful in healing.

While browsing in a stationery store, I found a card that showed a small boy pushing a wheelbarrow. The thing that caught my eye was the sheer joy on the child's face, and I was reminded of how long it had been since I felt that kind of joy. I bought the card and hung it in my office. Before I knew it, I was cutting out pictures of joyful people and plastering them all around. I soon started adding pictures of animals, family members, and all of the things that had once filled me with joy. And you know what? The pictures actually made me feel good. Instead of focusing on the gloom and doom in my life, the pictures helped me concentrate on the good things.

Set the scene for healing by surrounding yourself with pictures that make you laugh or smile. Hang fun sayings on your refrigerator door. This one from Miss Piggy always makes me laugh: "Never eat more than you can carry."

If you have young children, sit them down with magazines and scissors and have them make a collage of smiles. Hang it in a prominent place.

Set the stage for joy and laughter, and you set the stage for healing.

"Prepare the way for the Lord . . ."

(Mark 1:3)

The Language of Healing

Healing is not a cure; no cure exists for grief. Healing is a way of thinking, of being, of relating to the world. It's living each moment to the fullest. It's learning to draw upon inner strengths and responding to even our deepest troubles with appreciation, gratitude, and a new relationship with God.

Many patients with incurable diseases refuse to let the weakness of their bodies dictate who and what they are. By transcending the disease, they are, in essence, healed, no matter how physically ill they might be. With God's help, those of us who are in grief can be healed, too.

5

SPRING FEVER

Like a rambling rose,
I'm inching my way toward
my place in the sun.

We all know what the winter of grief is like; the cold, dark weeks and even months that follow the loss of a loved one. The icicles that touch the heart and soul. But did you know that grief also takes us through spring?

Spring fever hits sooner or later, and we begin to feel restless and impatient. If we have done the work of grief, sooner or later we will want to break out of our cocoon and move on with life. This feeling is normal, desirable, and what God intended.

But how do we start putting a shattered life back together? How do we even know where to start?

Start small. Start by taking an inventory of neglect. What have you neglected to do in recent months? What have you ignored?

"See! The winter is past; the rains are over and gone. Flowers appear on the earth; the season of singing has come . . ."
(Song of Solomon 2:11–12)

Grief can be tough on health. If you're like most people, health will be high on your list of neglect. During depression and grief, we can pack on as much as twenty pounds before we even realize it. Researchers tell us that losing as little as five pounds can make all of the difference in the world. Lose five pounds—just five pounds—and you'll be amazed at how your energy level increases and your aches and pains melt away. If you're overdue for a physical or a dental checkup, make an appointment.

Grief can be tough on finances. Sometimes we overspend in an effort to feel better. Start small. Make a budget, and start getting your finances under control by paying off one credit card or one outstanding bill.

Grief can be tough on relationships. We can be so involved in our own pain that we neglect friends and family, who may also be in pain. Start small. Invite one friend or family member to do something special with you.

Grief can be tough on the environment. Three years after my son's death, I realized that we had neglected the house. We had no heart for general maintenance or remodeling. Start small. Fix one leak or crack. Plan to paint or wallpaper one wall or room. Plant a single tree or weed one little corner of the yard.

Grief can be tough on spiritual matters. Start small. Ask for God's help. Attend a worship service. Visit a Christian bookstore. Reread your favorite scriptures. Spend time with a friend whose faith you admire.

Grief can be tough on appearances. We often neglect our wardrobe, even our hair. Treat yourself to a new outfit or hairdo. Open up the windows of your soul and let in the sunshine.

Reasons Why We Must Heal

- "I can't go back; I can't stay here; I must move forward."—Pastor Ray Pritchard
- "[P]assionate grief does not link us with the dead but cuts us off from them."—C.S.Lewis
- When grief takes center stage, God is pushed aside, and our life spins out of control. Healing begins when God becomes the center of our life.

"What the caterpillar calls the end, the master calls a butterfly."
—*Richard Bach*

6

SOUL WORK

My song of sorrow
is composed of deep feelings
my soul sings to me.

G rief pulls us back, slows us down, turns us inward until we come face to face with the spiritual self. We want to hide from our grief, from the raw reality of it, but the soul refuses to cooperate.

The soul seeks to grow, to question, and to understand, and this constant search plunges us into dangerous waters and hurls us into hostile space. It's the soul that demands answers from God.

"The soul is not a thing," Thomas Moore tells us in *Care of the Soul*. Rather it is "A quality or dimension of experiencing life and ourselves. It has to do with depth, value, relatedness, heart and personal substance."

Although sorrow at times seems to be the food of the soul, that's only an illusion. The reality is that a soul thrives on joy, seeking it like the roots of a tree seek moisture. Even during the darkest days of your grief, your soul is at work seeking answers, joy, and hope. And what the soul seeks, it eventually finds.

"Love the LORD your God with all your heart and with all your soul, and with all your strength."

(Deuteronomy 6:5)

7

STEPS TO REGAINING PASSION

I am relearning
old methods for these new times,
so I can move on.

W e see them all of the time—passionless people who are simply going through the motions of life, people who are burned out and used up and who have just plain given up.

Grief can at times make us feel empty, exhausted, depleted. After my own loss, I was convinced that my life was over. To survive, my soul needs passion and my heart needs joy, and I had lost both.

Fortunately, it was only a temporary loss. The passion and joy of living have since returned, but the highs are never quite as high as before; my joy is missing a wing. What once flew to great heights, now soars at a lower altitude, but that only makes the passions of my life that much more special and precious.

"You will make known to me the path of life; you will fill me with joy in your presence . . ."

(Psalm 16:11)

So how do we regain passion? How do we recapture the joy?

Refuse to Settle for a Life Without Passion.

In his insightful book *A Gift of Hope*, Robert Veninga insists that it's possible to learn to love life again, even when things go wrong. "You search and search and search," he writes, "until you find one person, one idea, one avocation that is so powerful that it penetrates the gloom."

Take Care of Your Spiritual Needs.

The Latin root word for spirituality, *spiritus*, means "breath," as in "breath of life." Recent research shows that something as simple as daily prayer or attending church can make you live longer—and happier.

Pursue Meaningful Goals.

If most of your time is spent pursuing activities that hold no meaning or joy for you, it's time to make changes, perhaps even a change of job.

Celebrate the Little Things.

I'll never forget the day I sold my first article. I received only five dollars, but it was a dream come true. To celebrate, my husband treated me to a dinner at an expensive restaurant. Not long after my first sale, I sold another article for *ten* dollars. Once again, my husband took me out to dinner. This time, however, when he looked at the check, he groaned and said, "I can't afford all this success." We still laugh about it, but the truth is that if I hadn't celebrated the little successes at the beginning of my career, I might never have stuck around long enough to see my name on a book. Celebrating the small successes maintains the passion.

Follow the Joy.

When we're living according to God's plan for us, we feel great joy. My passion for writing grew from the joy of putting words on paper. By following the joy, I found God's plan for me. In *The Wisdom of the Fathers*, Thomas Merton wrote, "By the taste of clear water, follow the brook to its source."

"You will make known to me the path of life; you will fill me with joy in your presence . . ."   *(Psalm 16:11)*

Healing Ways

Protect Your Immune System. Studies show that social outlets such as attending concerts and church and spending time with friends help to keep the immune system healthy.

A psalm of David.

The LORD is my shepherd, I shall not be in want.
He makes me lie down in green pastures,
He leads me beside quiet waters,
He restores my soul.
He guides me in paths of righteousness
for His name's sake.
Even though I walk
through the valley of the shadow of death,
I will fear no evil,
for you are with me;
your rod and your staff,
they comfort me.

Psalm 23:1–4

Healing Ways

The twenty-third psalm tells us that God cares for us, and will take care of our every need. This is especially true following the loss of a loved one. One way God takes care of us is through the wondrous healing process known as grief.

God gently slows us down in our grief, wrapping us in a dark cloak that makes us face the reality of our loss. Faith comes to us in quiet moments. The soul grows in stillness. The still waters of sadness prepare us for the next healing step.

God doesn't push us along the path of healing; he guides us through it, allowing us to heal in our own time, and in ways we never could imagine.

Though it is tempting to race through grief or ignore it altogether, the only way to fully heal is to *walk* through the valley of the shadow, holding on to God's hand every step of the way.

8

SEISMIC TREMORS

The seismic tremors
grief inflicts upon my world
leave me in chaos.

Grief affects every part of our personality, every thought or deed, every facet of our lives. The closer people live to the epicenter of our grief, the more seismic tremors they feel. The cashier feels seismic tremors when we fail to smile or be pleasant. Other drivers feel seismic tremors when our grief-stricken minds wander from the road. Our coworkers feel seismic tremors when we are withdrawn, depressed, or less productive than usual. Our friends feel seismic tremors when we pull away or refuse to let them help us. Our family feels seismic tremors when they hear us pacing the floor or see us succumbing to tears or staring into space.

The death of a loved one touches everyone we know. And, like anyone who has ever been in a natural disaster, they wait to see the all-clear sign—the smile, the word, the deed that signals that all is well with us.

Sometimes those signals are a long time in coming, and well-meaning friends try to hurry it along. "Aren't you over it yet?" they might say, or "It's been a year."

But only those who stand at the epicenter can know what it's like and how long it takes.

For those of us who are going through grief, it seems like an eternity.

For those who are feeling the seismic tremors, it seems like forever.

If we're not ready to signal the all clear, we can ask for more time. "I'm not ready, yet," we can say, or "Please be patient." Sometimes a simple thank you will do. "Thank you for standing by me through all of this."

Above all, be honest. Don't try to pretend that everything's okay when it's not. Dishonesty produces seismic tremors of its own.

"An honest answer is like a kiss on the lips."

(Proverbs 24:26)

9

A PLACE CALLED
DIARY

*My journal catches
the shattered bits of my life
neatly on straight lines.*

You won't find it on the map, but a diary is a place all the same, a place that allows us to dump, rail, cry, confess, pray, meditate, and explore. A diary is a place to grow, to try out different ideas, to dream. In a diary, we can take risks and chances.

In a diary, we can scream or cry, even laugh—freeing our souls, cleansing our hearts—and the pages will absorb our words without criticism, censure, or flinching. A diary is a place that is shockproof. It's a place without boundaries, a place without fences. It's as deep as our pain, as broad as our courage, and as wide as our imagination.

What would happen if every schoolchild was given fifteen minutes each morning to write in a diary? If every child had a place—a diary—in which to dump family problems, fears, anger, and bad dreams, would there be fewer discipline problems? Less violence? More openness to learning?

Those of us who are in grief need a dumping place. When our world has been turned upside down, we need to unload the guilt and anger and free ourselves from despair and confusion.

A diary is always open, twenty-four hours a day, seven days a week. When the world is asleep, we can go to this place, write in it, cry in it.

We must write deeply, dredging the bottom of our heart and the farthest reaches of our soul. In *The New Diary*, Tristine Rainer likens diary writing to deep-sea fishing and advises us to cast our lines as far and as deep as we can. "Don't stay close to the shore where the water is muddy," Rainer writes, "cast for your deepest thought or emotion."

Write fast from the soul; write slowly from the heart. Look for repetitive words or themes because they often lead to the source of a problem. One friend sat down to write about her mother's death and instead found herself writing about the father who had deserted the family when she was nine. "My diary made me realize that I had never dealt with the anger toward him, and my mother's death triggered unresolved feelings of loss and abandonment."

Write long; write short. Write fast; write slow. Don't be afraid of deep water. The fishing is great.

"See what large letters I use as I write to you with my own hand."
(Galatians 6:11)

10

EXPRESSING FEELINGS THROUGH ART

*Great inspiration
radiates from achievers
who've gone before us.*

Those who can't draw a straight line might feel intimidated by the very thought of drawing or painting. So many of us were programmed in childhood to draw *objects* as opposed to *feelings*. I still remember being told by an art teacher in second grade that my house didn't look like a house, and I was made to start over. The second drawing more closely resembled a structure, and, for that reason, won approval, but it lacked the emotional depth of the first picture.

When did we ever get the idea that art requires straight lines? How many straight lines do you see in Rembrandt's or da Vinci's work? Art, like nature, flows in swoops and swirls. Straight lines are for engineers.

Grief has no shape and no straight lines. It spins around us, through us, over us, and in us. No words exist that adequately describe it, but we can draw it.

So get out a box of crayons or water colors and start swirling. Let your grief spin across the page like falling leaves; let your feelings flow like rivers.

"In the beginning God created the heavens and the earth."

(Genesis 1:1)

Nurturing the Soul

Grief can be so dark and grim, so totally ugly. Is it any wonder that our soul shrinks back and turns away? It's the turning away that prevents our taking a closer look, finding God in the midst of despair, or being healed.

In *Care of the Soul*, Thomas Moore writes, "The soul is nurtured by beauty. What food is to the body . . . pleasing images are to the soul."

Fill your life with pleasing images.

- Surround yourself with cherished photos of family and friends.
- Fill a basket with fresh flowers, and give it to a shut-in.
- Spend an afternoon at an art museum, visit an old church, sit quietly in the park, browse through a bookstore, or listen to your favorite religious music.
- Walk beneath a star-filled sky; walk toward a sunset.
- Buy a yard of beautiful fabric and drape it over a lampshade, chair, or table top.
- Buy bright-colored sheets, paper a wall, or paint a door red.
- Do or say something that will make everyone you meet smile.

Feel the healing

11

VISIONS

*There's no way to know
which stage of our life will be
the most rewarding.*

When asked what she considered her best work of art, renowned sculptor Beatrice Wood, 102 years old at the time, pointed to a sculpture that she had done forty years earlier.

She explained that she could no longer remember the vision that she had had when she created the piece. Without the vision, she was finally able to judge the work on its own merits.

At the heart of all creativity is a vision. The need to create the vision is what keeps the writer writing, the artist striving. The vision must be significant enough to touch the inner depths of an artist's soul and large enough to assure failure. If I ever wrote the book that I envision, I would probably lose all desire to write another one. I would have completed my life's mission. It's the failure to create the vision that kept Rembrandt painting, Shakespeare writing, and Chopin composing. Most artists judge their work against the vision. Unable to see the beauty of their own creativity, they are often surprised when a work they have deemed a failure meets with critical acclaim.

Artists aren't the only ones blinded by a vision. We all have dreams that we chase. A baby is born, and the parents envision college and grandkids. A couple gets married, and they envision growing old together.

Following the death of a loved one, we tend to focus on what we had envisioned for our lives and often fail to appreciate the beauty that is left. One grieving mother admits that during her younger daughter's graduation from college, she kept thinking about the death of her oldest daughter and the graduation that she would never attend. "I was so miserable, I almost ruined my daughter's day."

There's beauty in life, even if we can't see it. In our darkest, deepest grief, we must believe in the beauty that still exists.

The future might not be the way you envisioned it, but with God's guiding light, it *can* be beautiful.

"Open my eyes that I may see wonderful things in your law."
                                                    (Psalm 119:18)

12

FIRST THINGS FIRST

We can surmount grief,
taking only baby steps,
if we keep going.

We live in a world of unwritten poems and unpainted landscapes. Many people dream of being a writer or an artist, but relatively few get around to putting pen or brush to paper, because they are too busy waiting for inspiration. The mistaken notion that inspiration precedes creativity has probably killed more dreams than lack of talent and skill combined.

Inspiration, the kind that sets you on fire, is rare. Writers are constantly asked where they get their ideas. Never will you hear a writer say, "I wait for them," because successful writers never wait; they go after ideas, sometimes with a pickax.

I've published more than twenty books, and I can count on one hand the number of times inspiration drove me to the computer. More often than not, I face a blank screen without the slightest idea what to write.

Inspiration comes from the work, seldom before it. I write before I *want* to write. Action precedes not only inspiration but also feelings. I wonder if it's possible to feel faithful to God without first *acting* faithful. If you never read the Bible or pray, is it possible to nurture the kind of faith that will carry you through trial and tribulation? I doubt it. Faith, like everything else, follows action.

Before we can heal, we must first *want* to heal. You'd be amazed at the number of people who prefer to wallow in pain rather than to work toward resolution and healing. The only difference between a victim and a survivor is action.

Plan a "do something" day, and you'll feel a whole lot better. If you want to . . .

- Feel inspired—create.
- Feel healthy—take a walk.
- Feel happy—laugh.
- Feel faithful—act faithful.
- Feel refreshed—cry.
- Feel friendship—be a friend.
- Feel hope—plan for the future.
- Feel good—do good.
- Feel love—show love.
- Feel appreciated—show gratitude.

"Even a child is known by his actions, by whether his conduct is pure and right."

(Proverbs 20:11)

13

CREATIVITY:
A ROAD TO GOD

*Each creative gift
transcends the darkness of death
to bring us comfort.*

When my daughter feels stressed out, she whips up a batch of cookies. When my husband needs to work out a problem, he tinkers in the garage. My personal stress buster is writing. During the weeks of my son's chemotherapy treatments, I sat in the waiting room, writing a book, controlling on paper that which could not be controlled in real life. Writing keeps me sane; it's the way I pray.

Other people pray through art or music. Some people create ways to calm the troubled soul through dance or by building houses, designing gardens, or arranging flowers.

Creativity can help express a passing emotion or a profound thought. It can reflect the beginning of a journey or the end of a quest. It can be the road to acceptance and discovery or a pleasant trail leading nowhere in particular. It can be a spiritual search or an emotional cleansing. It can be the means through which we talk to God.

Through creativity, we can glorify God, celebrate life, honor loved ones, and arrange the unacceptable, the unattainable, or the unbearable into manageable parts. Each time we create from the soul, we glorify God.

"Your hands shaped me and made me."

(Job 10:8)

14

HEALING THROUGH CREATIVITY

*Creativity
nurtures immortality
through our helping hands.*

Some people insist that they have no creative talents, but we are all made in the image of God—the source of all creativity. So why do so many people insist on something that can't possibly be true? Because it's safe; they think that denying talent frees them from the obligation of developing it. Creating works of art, whether building a model plane or writing a poem, opens us up to the world and possible criticism. The tendency is to hold back, to squelch the creative urges until we convince ourselves that none exist.

So creative talent lies dormant until such time that the need to create is greater than the fear of rejection. Often this time follows the death of a loved one.

Obituaries are filled with grief poems written by people who never wrote a poem before in their life. The AIDS project teems with quilts made by nonquilters. The Internet is crowded with eloquent prose written by grieving parents, spouses, and friends who insist that they can't write.

So the challenge today is to honor your loved one through creativity. Release your grief in a poem or a song. Arrange plants or flowers in a window box; build a birdhouse. Paint a room, cover a chair. Put together a scrapbook; fill a wall with photographs or posters that you love. Create an environment of caring.

Experience the joy and healing that comes when you let God work through your creative self.

"For we are God's workmanship, created in Christ Jesus to do good works . . ."

(Ephesians 2:10)

15

LEARNING FROM CHILDREN

When children's laughter
echoes through our living room,
I'm sure I hear you.

I remember telling my then-four-year-old daughter that some one she knew had died. She listened solemnly and said, "Don't worry, Mommy. He'll come alive again." She then explained how her favorite cartoon character came alive after falling off a cliff. Needless to say, we had a long talk.

The death of a loved one or even a pet can offer wonderful learning opportunities for children. Seeing his parents grieve teaches a child the value of life and the permanence of love.

By participating in the funeral, a child learns to express emotions in positive ways. A younger child might draw pictures of the loved one or help put together a scrapbook to be displayed at the funeral; an older child might read a Bible verse or share a special memory.

Children hearing adults openly discuss grief learn that it's okay to talk about feelings.

Children can learn many lessons about life and death by watching us grieve, but we can also learn from them. Children are blessed with a short attention span, meaning that they are able to balance grief with the joy of living. One mother told me how her own daughter reacted on the day of the funeral. "One moment my daughter was crying for her father and the next running through a field chasing a rabbit."

If it's been a while since you last ran through a field chasing rabbits, maybe it's time that you did.

"And a little child will lead them."

(Isaiah 11:6)

16

THE HEALING POWER OF MUSIC

The sound of music
possesses soothing powers
that mend broken hearts.

It's been known since ancient times that music has the power to heal. Early man believed that illness was caused by the loss of inner harmony. Even Hippocrates, the father of medicine, treated mentally ill patients with music. The German poet Novalis went so far as to state that *every* illness is a musical problem.

Those of us who are in grief have a musical problem. Not only has the harmony of heart and soul been disrupted but we also feel out of tune with the world around us.

When the music has left our soul, it helps to seek other sources. For example, Ida joined the church choir after her daughter's death and found comfort in making music for others to enjoy.

Classical music helped Jim following the death of his wife. Connecting to the great composers through their music inspired him to seek out ways to stay connected to his wife.

Mary says that every time she feels especially low in spirit, she flips on the radio and inevitably hears the song that she and her husband claimed as their own. "It always puts a smile on my face."

Not just any music heals; jazz and rock tend to make the heart lose its normal rhythm. Studies show that plants that are exposed to rock music often die within a month, but plants that are exposed to Bach can grow as much as three inches higher than even those that are kept in silence.

In his book *The Secret Power of Music*, David Tame writes, "Every moment of music to which we subject ourselves may be enhancing or taking away our life energies and clarity of consciousness, increment by increment."

Music that heals and soothes is the same tempo as the heartbeat. So surround yourself with Bach, Brahms, and Beethoven. Let your heart beat to Mozart. Let Handel and Strauss set the tempo of your soul. Enhance your life by letting the healing power of the Masters solve the musical problem of grief.

"Sing to the LORD with thanksgiving; make music to our God on the harp."

(Psalm 47:7)

Healing Ways

God loves music, and He commands even nature to sing songs of praise, joy, and thanksgiving. Music can bring us to tears or make us laugh. It can lift the spirits, help us sleep, and soothe the weary soul. We can block out the world in our grief and sorrow, but we cannot block out the music of God's world.

17

MUSIC OF THE SOUL

Life is a concert
we must conduct with our own
rhythm and tempo.

As a child, I took piano lessons from an animated German man named Mr. Frantz. Nothing got him more incensed than my failure to hold a rest for its full count. "Don't you understand?" he bellowed more times than I care to remember. "There is music in the silence."

I never questioned his wisdom until I lost my son. Family, friends, and coworkers are the chords from which we compose the symphony of our lives, the instruments through which we make our music heard. When we lose a loved one, we lose part of our orchestra, and the silence that remains can be devastating.

Eventually, the music of life flows again. The sound is different, so is the rhythm, and we might find ourselves stumbling over unfamiliar notes, but with practice comes skill.

If you've yet to find music in the silence, improvise. Hang wind chimes in your yard to catch the sound of the slightest breeze. Put up a bird feeder and rejoice in the happy sounds of nature. Place a water fountain on your desk and let the sound of running water soothe your soul. Let each room of your house sing with its own music.

The loss of a loved one creates a silence in our lives, a pause in the rhythm, but those who wish to sing will always find a song. The song composed by grief, though deeper and more haunting than earlier songs, can still be beautiful, perhaps even more beautiful and meaningful than before. All you have to do is want to sing.

Music for the Grieving Soul

To release bottled-up feelings: Try listening to blues or country-western.

If you're having trouble sleeping: Slow classical music with the same 60—to 79-beats per minute as the resting heart can often do the trick. Try Handel's *Water Music* or Pachelbel's *Canon in D.*

If you're having trouble concentrating: The right music can activate the brain and help clarify thinking. The mathematical structure of Mozart's music seems to resonate with the brain. Try Mozart's Allegro from *Violin Concerto #3*

If you're feeling anxious: Gospel music can be comforting and inspirational.

If you're feeling depressed: Lively show tunes or patriotic music can lift the spirits.

"Sing to the LORD, all the earth; proclaim his salvation day after day."
(1 Chronicles 16:23)

18

THE COLOR OF GRIEF

Grief is a black veil
that obscures our vision of
the world's true colors.

Color doesn't occur in the world, Diane Ackerman tells us, "but in the mind." Colors are brightest when we are in love or feel joy or happiness. If we are depressed or grieving, we see the world in black and white or shades of gray.

One widow friend said she knew that she was on the road to recovery when the first thing she noticed one morning was a bright red rose outside her window.

Colors affect our emotions. Certain colors even stimulate the appetite, and that's why restaurants are often painted in shades of red or orange. Red has also been proven to make us physically stronger. Green or blue are soothing colors; pink is thought to be nurturing.

Black, the color we most readily associate with grief, is the color that is hardest to find in its purest form. Black is not really a color but a combination of many colors. Black is a winter color because it best absorbs heat from the sun. I like to think that black also absorbs the caring feelings of others. Perhaps that is why we wear it at funerals and when we're feeling depressed or vulnerable. Sometimes, though, black can be a sad reminder that all is not right with our world.

So why, then, do we surround ourselves in black when we grieve? Is it because the colors that comprise black best express the many emotions we feel? The anger? The sadness? The loneliness? Or is it because we seek to protect ourselves from what suddenly seems like a hostile world, much like Mother Nature uses black as camouflage to protect wildlife.

Do we wear black to express our emotions, or is it a cry for help? Does black protect and warm us, or do we use it as a shield?

Look around. How bright are the colors in your world? Has the time come to don the colors of love and happiness, to surround ourselves with colors that celebrate the lasting gifts our loved ones left us?

Wear something bold red—as a reminder of your fortitude. Snuggle up in baby pink. Buy a yellow rose—a symbol of courage. Take a walk on lush green grass. Treat yourself to a box of crayons and invite a child to help you break them in. Wear your loved one's favorite color. Wear the color you think best represents recovery and hope.

Shed the mantle of grief, and you'll find a world of rainbows waiting for you.

> *"Like the appearance of a rainbow in the clouds on a rainy day, so was the radiance around him."*
>
> (Ezekiel 1:28)

19

HEALING THROUGH BEAUTY

When a balloon bursts,
there is sadness all around
for the beauty lost.

Beauty puts a face on God. When we gaze at nature, at a loved one, or at a work of art, our soul immediately recognizes and is drawn to the face of God.

Plotinus wrote, "When it [the soul] sees anything of that kin, or any trace of that kinship, it thrills with an immediate delight, takes its own to itself, and thus stirs anew to the sense of its nature and all its affinity."

It's hard to see the face of God in our grief. It's possible that Plotinus was referring to grief when he wrote, "But let the soul fall in with the Ugly and at once it shrinks within itself, denies the thing, turns away from it, . . . resenting it."

Grief can be so dark and grim, so totally ugly. Is it any wonder that our souls shrink back and turn away? It's the turning away that prevents us from taking a closer look, from finding God in the midst of despair—from healing.

It's only when we look ugly in the face that we begin to see a different picture. The pain in our heart is not a knife or sword, as we might imagine, but love that has no place to go.

The darkness of grief is not a shroud but a protector, allowing the wounds of heart and soul to heal without the glare of a hostile world.

The silence of grief is not punishment but a gift, allowing us to hear the whispers of the heart and the voice of God.

Look for beauty in every aspect of your life; see the face of God.

"[H]e sees God's face and shouts for joy."

(Job 33:26)

20

FRESH GRIEF

As I travel on,
my path is steeper without
God as my compass.

The winding mountain trail seemed to go on forever.. Hot and tired, I was about to turn back when I met two hikers coming the other way. "How far to the waterfalls?" I called. "About half a mile," one man replied.

Half a mile! I couldn't believe it. There was no way that I could manage another half mile. Apparently, one of the hikers sensed my dismay. "The falls are beautiful," he called, "and you've already covered the hardest part of the trail."

Encouraged, I trudged on, and the falls *were* beautiful. Had it not been for those two hikers, I would have given up. If I had met them earlier, when I first started out, and found out how difficult the climb was, I might never have made it to the top.

Those of us who are in grief don't need anyone to tell us the conditions of the trail ahead. We don't want to know, and we reject, even resent, reports of splendor down the road. "You'll be a better person," one grieving mother told me. Who cares? I wanted to yell. "I don't want to be a better person."

"You'll be happy again," a grieving father said, and I wanted to scream, "Are you crazy? I will *never* be happy again."

"You'll find peace," a widow told me, and everything inside me protested. How can I find peace when everything I once believed in is now suspect, even God?

Fresh grief is no time to find good in the bad. We don't want to know that the view is great or that wonderful things lie ahead. It's hard to see the view when you're blinded by tears. Nor should we try to sort out feelings about God and faith when we can't even determine night from day.

Fresh grief is a time to sit on the trail and cry, to sob our hearts out, to tell our story, and to feel the pain.

If it's been only days or weeks since your loved one died, you're probably not ready to think in terms of gifts and blessings. This is normal, and it means that you're still working your way through the acute grieving process.

Once you are ready to proceed along the trail of grief, you'll welcome, even search out reports on conditions ahead. You might even find yourself tempted to give reports to those who are trailing behind.

"Show me your ways, O LORD, teach me your paths."
(Psalm 25:4)

Healing Ways

Matthew 29–30 tells us that Jesus went up a mountainside, sat down, and healed everyone who came to Him. It couldn't have been easy for the crippled and blind people to journey up a mountain, but it was a necessary part of the healing process.

God heals those who want to be healed. He heals those who reach out to Him and who follow His laws.

So don't be afraid to climb the mountain of despair; don't hesitate to walk through the valley of darkness because that's where you'll find God's loving comfort.

Let each day unfold
like the petals of a rose,
high above the thorns.

21

Mining the Grieving Soul

Each life is a mine,
wherein we carefully seek
our golden moments.

I love the process of writing a book. The planning and research-
ing are as important to me as the actual writing.

Paying my bills is another process that gives me pleasure, partly
because I remember the time when I was poor. Writing out checks
for utilities and mortgage payments reminds me of how blessed I
am to have so much. For this reason, I resist the idea of paying
bills electronically.

I have to admit that on some level, grief intrigues me. Not that
it's something that I would ever choose to go through voluntarily.
Grief brings out our human side, our vulnerability. But it also brings
out the best that we have to give because grief is the pouring out of
unconditional love for another person.

Although it's tempting to hurry through grief, it's important to
mine it for all possible treasures. The process of grief is a process
of discovery. We will probably learn more about ourselves, about
our faith and strengths, and about our friends and family during
grief than at any other time in our life.

Keep writing, reading, listening, and praying. Tackle grief with the openmindedness of a scholar and the curiosity of a chemist. *Thar's gold in them thar hills!*

"But store up for yourselves treasures in heaven . . ."
                                        (Matthew 6:20)

22

WHEN I SAY YOUR NAME . . .

You are my sunshine,
even though you aren't here
to brighten my day.

O h, wouldn't Kevin laugh at me now? My daughter, an exhausted and overwhelmed first-time mother of a newborn at the time, laughed as she said it, and I laughed, too. The most organized person in our family was still in her nightgown at three o'clock in the afternoon, and the house was a disaster. I could almost hear her brother's teasing voice—we both could—but rather than depress us, it lifted our spirits.

Saying a loved one's name without getting emotional takes time. But when raw grief has mellowed into a more manageable sadness, saying a loved one's name will be like lighting a candle in the dark of night.

When we say the name naturally and lovingly, we let others know that it's okay to talk about the loved one or share a memory about them. Children, especially, are quick to pick up on subtle signals. If they sense that a subject is off limits, or that their parents are holding back, they'll internalize their grief.

So, go ahead, become a name dropper. It's good for the soul.

"The LORD is his name."

(Exodus 15:3)

23

GIFTS FROM THE SEA

Strolling down the beach,
I shed my grief for the tide
to carry away.

The first stage of grief is an angry ocean, tossing us about like corks in the churning depths. Grief pounds us with wave after wave of emotion until our chest hurts, and we literally gasp for air. Grief pulls us into the deepest abyss of darkness and despair, until we give up any hope of ever reaching shore.

Then something happens. We see an island of hope, and we start swimming with renewed energy. Grief loosens its grip, and we pick ourselves up, only to be knocked over by another wave. Gradually, the waves taper off, and we learn to anticipate them. We know that a wave will hit on a certain holiday or a certain birthday, but practice makes perfect, and, over time, we learn to ride the waves with the grace of a surfer.

Eventually, we wash up on shore for good, but we never venture far from the ocean's grasp. In his book *Suicide and Life-Threatening Behavior*, Edwin Shneidman writes, "The figurative sands of secondary grief stay on the beaches of our psyches all the remainder of our lives."

So what gifts are found in the sea of grief? What lessons can be gleaned from the depths?

In her book *Gift From the Sea*, Anne Morrow Lindbergh wrote that the sea teaches us openness.

This is true of grief. Cracks in a building allow sun and air to enter. Broken hearts and shattered spirits open us up to God.

The sea of grief also reveals inner strengths, allowing us to swim out farther than we ever thought possible. We now know that we can survive the most harrowing depths, the most dangerous storms, the most threatening waves. There's freedom and peace of mind, even a sense of joy, in knowing of what one is capable.

The sea of grief also teaches us to value and cherish our lifesavers. In the depths of despair, we hold on to faith, friends, and family until one or all pulls us out of the depths.

It helps to wander around the beach for awhile, to skirt the edge of grief, relishing the gift of life and the new opportunities that lie ahead like so many shells on the sand. But we dare not linger too long because, as Anne Morrow Lindbergh reminds us, "There are other beaches to explore. There are more shells to find. This is only a beginning . . ."

"So they pulled their boats up on shore, left everything and followed Him."

(Luke 5:11)

24

THE GIFT OF STORYTELLING

I feel like Aesop
in search of receptive ears
to hear my stories.

Our youngest son had the habit of whispering following his nightly bath. We'd hear him in his room, whispering to his toys, convinced that if we couldn't hear him we'd forget that it was his bedtime. Sometimes, his little ploy worked, and we *did* forget, at least for a short time.

During the weeks before my older son's death, we spoke in whispers. I wonder if, deep down, we hoped that by being quiet we would fool the angel of death into passing us by.

We whisper in the presence of death or at funerals. We whisper when we are afraid, ashamed, or feel unsure of ourselves.

My friend Sally whispers whenever she talks of the brother who died when she was seven. She explains that no one was allowed to talk about him and so, even today, thirty-five years later, she feels guilty for even mentioning his name and can do so only in the softest of voices.

My grandchildren constantly clamor for stories of the "olden days." "Tell us about the time Uncle Kevin got stuck behind the toilet," they beg in loud voices. "Tell us how Great Grandpa Brownley had to change his name at Ellis Island." The children keep all of these names straight because of the photo gallery in our hall. Each photo is labeled. One such label reads "Christine Gehbauer, a Red Cross nurse in World War I."

Moses told his stories around a campfire in the wilderness. Jesus used parables to teach life lessons. We can all be better teachers by following His model. If we keep the memories of our deceased relatives alive through the stories we tell, we give our children a sense of belonging and teach them that death is a natural part of life, and our loved ones stay in the heart forever.

"Tell us about Great, Great Grandmother Lulu!" the oldest of my grandchildren pleads. No whispers there!

"Jesus spoke all these things to the crowd in parables; he did not say anything to them without using a parable."

(Matthew 13:34)

Following Jesus' Example

Open your family treasure chest, and let the stories take on new life. Pick out your favorite memory, and let it wrap itself around you like a warm blanket. Share your stories with someone over tea or dinner. Write them in a journal or on the back of family photos. Start a "Family Story" file on your computer and invite everyone to share a favorite tale. Record your stories on a tape recorder or video for future generations. Stitch your story into a quilt. Relish and enjoy your stories as many times as you wish. Feel the healing.

25

FOOTPRINTS IN THE SAND

The sound of a wave
joyfully kissing the shore
tranquilizes me.

As I walk upon the sands of grief, I'm reminded of a sign posted at the entrance of a national park: "Leave only footprints and take nothing but photographs."

It's a sign that could be posted on the gates of heaven. For aren't footprints what our loved ones leave behind? Footprints that we try to fill. Footprints that sink deep into our hearts. Footprints that forever change who and what we are.

In my grief, I realize that I haven't made many footprints lately. I've been too caught up in my own sorrow to make much of an imprint in anyone else's life, even my own.

I like to think that when we die, we take our memories with us because memories are the photographs of the soul. But what memories have I created in recent months? I've been too busy dwelling on old memories to think about creating new ones.

But the death of a loved one teaches us that life is short, and we have only so much time to create footprints and memories for those whom we must one day leave behind.

Make today significant by creating footprints in someone's heart. Create a memory by doing something fun with a person you love. Lives are measured by the footprints and memories left behind. Don't be caught short.

"I thank my God every time I remember you."

(Philippians 1:3)

"Creating like unto our Divine Master is the only way of rising toward God."

(Paul Gauguin)

26

VITALITY BEGUN

Cherish this moment,
for it will be quickly gone,
never to return.

Grief provides a minefield of endless possibilities. We grieve loss but gain a better appreciation of those around us. We grieve death and find life.
Emily Dickinson wrote,

A death blow is a life blow to Some who till they died, did not alive become—who had they lived, had died but when they died, Vitality begun.

The reality of death teaches us how short and how precious life is. It teaches us to live more fully in the moment, to make the most of each bright new day, to choose more carefully how we use our time and with whom to spend it. The death of a loved one makes us more cautious in word, more generous in deed, and more profound in thought. Death forces us to look inward, to question and to grow. Death forces us to look outward, to learn and to give.

Death turns us inside out and upside down, turns us into a potboiler of emotions. In Dickinson's words, "Vitality begun . . ."

"I was blind but now I see!"

(John 9:25)

27

ART IS FOR HEALING

*The talents we hone
throughout life determine the
gifts we leave behind.*

When was the last time you dumped the closets of the soul onto an empty canvas? When did you last pour the contents of your heart into a slab of clay? Art provides the freedom to empty the heart and soul without words. Art is the dumping ground of the spirit.

In her book *The Artist's Way*, Julia Cameron writes, "Art opens the closets, airs out the cellars and attics. It brings healing . . ."

To create art in any form requires faith. In *Creative Spirit*, authors Daniel Goleman, Paul Kaufman and Michael Ray wrote, "When people have faith in their creativity, they demonstrate a clarity of purpose that will startle those around them."

If the thought of creating a work of art scares you, start with a brand new box of crayons. Don't worry about drawing anything specific. Instead, scribble away your anger with black or purple, crowd out your loneliness with red or orange. Let your sadness spill out in shades of blue. Let a little sunshine stream through with splotches of yellow.

Startle your friends with your faith.

"He put a new song in my mouth . . ."

(Psalm 40:3)

God, the Refiner

"He will sit as a refiner and purifier of silver."

(Malachi 3:3)

A story floating around the Internet tells of a woman who went to a silversmith in an attempt to understand how this verse defined God. The silversmith held a piece of silver in the flames and explained that this process burned away the impurities. He then explained the importance of watching the silver at all times during the refinement process. Silver left too long in the fire would be destroyed.

The woman asked how he knew when the silver had been refined, and the silversmith replied, "That's easy—when I see my image."

28

THE HEALING POWER OF NATURE

*The Creator's plan
guarantees to give the world
continuity.*

In 1980, a volcanic eruption turned the beautiful forests and sparkling clear waters of Mount St. Helens into a lunar waste land. Today, the area flourishes with new vegetation and teems with animal life.

We can learn a lot by watching nature heal. Trees from more than two hundred miles of forest were blown into Spirit Lake, and the churning logs filtered ashes and sulfur out of the water. Once the waters had been cleansed, recovery began.

The barren wasteland remaining after a volcanic eruption is all too familiar to those of us who are in grief. The world is without color and beauty; the days stretch before us like a black hole. We feel lifeless, dead. Sometimes we feel so depressed that we don't even notice the first signs of healing.

God heals in stages, according to priorities. During a crisis, physical needs take precedence over spiritual and mental needs. During the first few weeks following the death of a loved one, we are in shock, and our senses are numb. This is God's way of protecting us. But it's only a temporary measure. No recovery can occur while we are in that state; soon the shock wears off, and we feel the full impact of our loss. Although it might not seem possible, healing has actually begun.

Once the senses are restored, the ability to smell and taste triggers the appetite. Blood vessels relax, regulating body heat, and we no longer feel cold. The pulse becomes normal again, and the headaches and nausea leave us. No longer dulled by shock, our auditory and visual senses work to bring order to a chaotic world. Although this increases our pain by making us even more aware of our loss, it's a necessary step toward healing.

Some of the most beautiful parts of the world were created by the destructive forces of a volcano. Tragedies and losses have turned even ordinary people into extraordinary human beings. The horrendous grief that gripped Europe during the bubonic plague, the dreaded "Black Death," was followed by the magnificent Renaissance.

Although the landscape of our soul seems to have been stripped bare, God in His wisdom finds a seed of faith from which to work, a thread of hope from which to build, a part that seeks to find the sunlight, and so begins the healing process.

God's healing love can nourish the darkest soul and change even the most barren landscape into a thing of beauty.

"God is our refuge and strength, an ever-present help in trouble. Therefore we will not fear, though the earth give way and the mountains fall into the heart of the sea . . ."

(Psalm 46:1–2)

Healing Ways

Grief creates in us a need to start over, to change the way we do things, and to seek a more mature faith, a more meaningful life, and more loving relationships. God challenges us to change and to grow by creating new things.

"Sing to him a new song." (Psalm 96:1)

"Therefore, if anyone is in Christ, he is a new creation." (2 Corinthians 5:17)

"What counts is a new creation." (Galatians 6:15)

"Be made new in the attitude of your minds." (Ephesians 4:23)

Change, grow, seek, create—feel the healing.

The song in my heart
my friends long to hear me sing
is caged up by grief

29

TURN OFF THE NOISE

The sound of the wind
whispering through the treetops
is God's lullaby.

The deafening roar of life is static from the information age. The TV, radio, Internet, and newspapers bombard us with the latest news. It's hard to escape the parade of financial wizards who are only too glad to voice their opinions. The medical experts keep us on a physical roller coaster.

Eat fat; don't eat fat. Buy stocks; don't buy stocks. Drink coffee; don't drink coffee. Such static is enough to make you want to hide in a cave.

Even grief offers no respite. As Shakespeare pointed out, everyone's an expert—except those who grieve. Friends and acquaintances, even those who have never lost a loved one, are not shy in doling out advice. We're told when we should date again, get on with our lives, and stop "feeling sorry for ourselves."

The best way to deal with the "roar" is to tune it out. The TV news is off limits in our house. I no longer purchase magazines that make me dissatisfied with my appearance or housekeeping skills. No longer do I feel guilty for not making my own gifts or failing to turn my husband into a nonstop lover.

As for grief, we turn out the static there, too. We surround ourselves with the "real" experts—the people who have suffered a loss such as ours.

When we turn off the static, we hear the sounds of nature. When we tune out the hype, we hear words of love. When we block out criticism, we can listen to words of praise. When we turn off the world, we can then focus on the voice of God.

"The voice of the LORD is powerful; the voice of the LORD is majestic."
(Psalm 29:4)

30

THE HEALING EARTH

The world keeps changing,
swapping old spirits for new
continuously.

It's possible to go for weeks, even months, without touching the earth. We scurry about on cement, toil away in steel buildings, travel in cars or trains. Even children have less contact with the earth today than they did in previous generations. Most school playgrounds are covered in asphalt, and children are more likely to be found in front of the TV than climbing trees or running through the grass.

We are all connected to one another through Mother Earth. When we distance ourselves from the earth, our world becomes too small, our vision too limited, and our lives too self-centered. To touch the earth is to touch all of life, both past and present. The earth helps us put things in perspective and reminds us that we are all connected.

We find comfort in the earth's rhythm, much as a baby finds comfort in its mother's heartbeat. When we sleep, our brain waves match the gentle tremors of the earth, and this phenomenon could explain the healing and restorative properties of sleep. In *A Natural History of the Senses*, Dianne Ackerman writes, "Dreaming, we become the earth's dream."

Our emotions are linked to the earth; we respond to the wind and the rain, to the ebb and flow of the ocean, to the changing seasons.

Touch the earth with hands and feet; touch it with heart and soul. Let your emotions ride the wind; let your spirit climb a mountain. Build a snowman; hug a tree. Walk barefoot in the grass; run across the sand. Touch the flowers, pick a rose, or plant a seed. Climb a rock; skip a pebble. Catch a raindrop; let the sun warm your skin.

Dream the dreams of the earth.

"For God is the King of all the earth; sing to him a psalm of praise."
(Psalm 47:7)

Healing Ways

"Praise him, sun and moon, praise him, all you shining stars."
(Psalm 148:3)

Listen to the wind, to the song of birds. Listen to the tall trees, the rippling grass, the sound of a babbling brook. Listen to all of nature praise God.

Feel the healing.

31

THE HEALING GARDEN

*When living tributes
set new roots and sprout new growth,
dead spirits grow, too.*

Man's first home was a garden. After God created heaven and earth, He made a garden home to Adam and Eve. Perhaps this explains why so many of us are drawn to the garden in times of grief and sorrow. Even Jesus sought refuge in a garden during His darkest hour.

Gardens keep us in touch with the cycle of life. Birth, life, death, hope, love, faith, and God are all necessary for a successful garden.

A good gardener knows that plants, like family and friends, must be cared for daily. Neglect a garden, and it will die.

Like a child, a garden requires both restriction and freedom. A gardener must be flexible; if we try to grow a garden exactly as envisioned, it will never reach its full potential. Vines must wander occasionally, and trees must be allowed to bend to suit their natures, the same as grief.

A garden can be planted in a box or spread over acres of land. It can hang from baskets or cover a roof. A garden can be as big or as small as circumstances permit.

Plant a butterfly garden, a cactus, an herb, or a Bible garden. Design a Shakespearean, Monet, or da Vinci garden. Plant a shadow or shade garden, a water, sun, or secret garden. Plant a passionate purple garden, a garden of rainbows, a Japanese garden. Plant a memorial garden, filling it with your loved one's favorite flowers.

Salute the past with a heritage garden. Plan a rose garden.

Fill your garden with birdbaths and feeding stations—all of the things that will further connect you to nature. Plant a garden; plant a refuge; plant a *home.*

"I am the true vine, and my Father is the gardener."

(John 15:1)

32

CAN'T STOP CRYING

Losing a loved one
is life's whitewater trip on
a river of tears.

We cry at weddings or when a child is born. Some movies make us cry; certain songs make us teary-eyed. We cry when we're happy or when we're sad. We cry when we lose someone we love.

A Native American proverb states, "If the eyes had no tears, the soul would have no rainbows."

Tears of sadness differ chemically from tears of joy, because they stem from different emotions. On the practical side, tears cleanse the body and clean the eyes; on a more spiritual side, they release overwrought emotions and refresh the soul.

It's been said that women cry five times more than men, and for this reason some people think that crying is a sign of weakness.

Not so, according to Washington Irving, who wrote, "There is a sacredness in tears. They are not the mark of weakness, but of power. They speak more eloquently than ten thousand tongues. They are the messengers of overwhelming grief, of deep contrition, and of unspeakable love."

We all react to a loss in different ways. Not everyone cries; some people grieve deeply without shedding a single tear. Others cry sporadically or nonstop for days or weeks on end.

Nothing is wrong with any of these responses to loss; some souls simply need more rainbows than others.

"Jesus wept."

(John 11:35)

If you cry a lot: Chances are you're not expressing feelings verbally. Tears are a great emotional release, but healing comes through talking, not crying.

If you cry hardly at all: A good cry will provide an emotional release and make you feel less stressed. Rent a sad movie to get you started.

33

PROMISE OF A RAINBOW

*We search for rainbows,
but we must weather a storm
before we see one.*

A group of us get together from time to time to houseboat on Lake Powell. It took three trips before we managed to explore the entire two thousand miles of shoreline. During our first two trips, we had "perfect" weather. Toward the end of the third trip, our luck ran out, and it rained. We pulled into a little cove for the night, hoping that the storm would be gone by morning.

That night, white streaks of lightning danced upon the mountaintops and zigzagged into the rugged canyons. It was a spectacular sight but nowhere near as spectacular as the sight that greeted us the next morning: the water, having gathered in gullies high above us, gushed down the mountainsides, surrounding us with no fewer than twenty-eight waterfalls. The view was breathtaking and one that we would have missed had we experienced only "good" weather.

Rain provides color and texture to the world; it clears the air and provides an environment for growth. After days of rain, the sky is bluer, the grass is green, and even the air sparkles. Without rain, there can be no rainbows.

Grief seems like a storm that will never end; it's the worst possible kind of storm that drenches our spirit and batters our soul. Just when it seems that we are about to drown in the torrential rains of pain and depression, a rainbow appears.

Jeanna's rainbow came in the form of a new love in her life whom she met at a bereavement group. "I never thought I'd love again," she explained.

Marty's rainbow was joining the Peace Corps. "After my husband died, I wanted to do something meaningful with my life."

Take a walk following a spring rain. Read the story of Noah's ark to a child. Hang sun catchers or glass prisms in a window. Make a birthday cake for someone, decorating it with a rainbow. Wrap a gift with rainbow paper. Delight a child by making rainbows with a hose. Blow bubbles outside, and watch the rainbow colors as the bubbles drift away. Fulfill a promise you made to someone, perhaps your loved one. Fly a rainbow flag.

Today, look for rainbows in your life. Look for the promise of good things to come. Look for messages from God. Look for signs of recovery.

"I have set my rainbow in the clouds, and it will be the sign of the covenant between me and the earth."

(Genesis 9:13)

The Bible begins and ends with a rainbow, and each time God uses the rainbow as a sign of new beginnings, a promise of better things to come.

34

AUTUMN LEAVES

Autumn colors are
God's beautiful tribute to
dying foliage.

Grief makes us want to pull back, pull in, and hold tight to whatever is left. A better way, perhaps, would be to use God's model for healing and growth—nature. Autumn is the time when the blossoms of last summer are let go, released, and discarded. It's how nature prepares the way for new foliage in the spring.

Let the "leaves" of old dreams fall away, and you'll make room for the new. Release the pain, and you'll allow for new growth. Prune away old goals, and new ones will take flight. Give up the life once planned, and another life, a different yet no less wondrous life, will unfold.

Give up, release, and let go until the bare branches of your soul are exposed in preparation for a glorious spring.

"He cuts off every branch in me that bears no fruit, while every branch
that does bear fruit He prunes so that it will be even more fruitful."
                                                                    (John 15:2)

*Thank God for the gifts
He has given directly
or via loved ones.*

35

DISCOVERY THROUGH GRIEF

The meaning of life
can be understood only
by accepting death.

During a trip to Kansas, I drove past miles of monotonous grasslands, anxious to reach my destination. Only after pulling over to the side of the road to stretch my travel-weary bones did I discover the grandeur and beauty of the prairie.

The scent of damp earth and wild flowers lifted my spirits and melted away my exhaustion. The song of birds, rising from the rippling grass, revived my road-dead brain; the wind whispering through the tall dancing stalks seemed to call to me. Walking through the grass that reached high above my head, I marveled at the vast variety of insects and complicated structure of flowers, leaves and stems that lived beneath the green canopy.

Like the traveler who races through prairie or desert, many of us journey through life oblivious to its beauty. We rush through the days, cramming each hour with frantic activity, while missing the little things that make life worth living. Most of us would still be racing through life had the death of a loved one not stopped us in our tracks.

Bound by the pain and anguish of grief, we can only focus on what's up close. The here and now. Things that we took for granted or otherwise ignored take on new dimensions. Money, career, success, and material things no longer hold meaning for us.

Grief magnifies even the smallest areas of our life. This fact helps us gain a new appreciation for the people about whom we care, the things that are important to us, the wonders of nature. Is it even possible to look at God's world, to study the structure and patterns of all living things, and not gain a deeper faith in the Creator? I doubt it. Nor is it possible to focus on a loved one without growing in love and understanding.

Take a walk in the woods or desert with a magnifying glass. Stop to study the bark on the trees, the tracings in the sand, the shape of each flower.

Walk through your house and touch all of the things that you hold dear. Focus on the people in your life, and tell each one what makes them so special to you.

Walk down a street you normally drive. Take a child on a tour of your house and explain the meaning behind the things you love. Even your own children might not know that the clock on the wall was a wedding gift from Aunt Susan. Putter in your garden, and cup each flower in your hands. Stand still and wrap yourself in the beauty of God's world.

"Pay attention and gain understanding."

(Proverbs 4:1)

36

AM I LOSING MY MIND?

Grief's bizarre feelings
boggle my understanding
of what's wrong with me.

Sarah-Sue thought that she was losing her mind when she walked into the house and smelled her husband's aftershave. Chester swears that he saw his dead wife in a crowd. Lydia thought that she'd gone over the edge when she called her deceased son to dinner.

Am I losing my mind? This is a question that many of us ask ourselves during our grief journey, especially in the early months. Even our friends might wonder at some of our bizarre behavior. But, as we all know by now, death changes the rules of behavior: bizarre is normal; normal is crazy. And the world is upside down.

It's been said that those who can't hear the music think that the dancer is mad. Only those of us who have lost a loved one and danced the dance of grief can understand.

Lisa thought that she was going crazy when she sat in a trancelike state for hours on end. Jim worried about his sudden obsession with obituaries. Camryn kept reliving mentally the final moments of her mother's life.

If you think that you're losing your mind, then everything is perfectly normal. Call on the Lord's help to lead you through the maze of confusion. Enjoy the music while it lasts.

Grief's pathway to peace
travels up, down, and across
a river of tears.

37

WHAT IS THIS THING CALLED GRIEF?

Life challenges me,
slapping me with your demise,
the duel is mine.

The nature of grief pulls us away from the world, binding us to the heart and soul until we regain strength and courage.

The tears shed in grief allow for crystal-clear vision, illuminating friends and family through wiser, more loving eyes.

The darkness of grief allows us to follow even the dimmest light of faith to the source of all hope.

The stillness of grief is an invitation to sail into the inner self and explore the harbor of forgotten goals and still-cherished dreams.

The reality of grief helps us find new purpose and meaning in life, a new reason for being.

The permanence of grief is reassuring. Experiencing grief and seeing others grieve tells us that we will not be forgotten after death. This, in turn, encourages us to live our lives and relate to others in ways that will benefit loved ones and influence lives long after we're gone.

"Listen to me; be silent, and I will teach you wisdom."

(Job 33:33)

Angels unaware
are set carefully in place
by a loving God.

"Above all else, guard your heart,
for it is the wellspring of life."
(Proverbs 4:23)

PART THREE

Healing the Grieving Heart

Society's Way:
Grieve alone.

God's Way:
Grieve with the help of family and friends.

Introduction to Part 3

Broken hearts can heal
with their love and hope intact
when grieving God's way.

We feel confused, alone, and afraid. Consumed by anger and guilt, we pull back and withdraw. Our chest fills with a pain so sharp that it literally takes our breath away. These are signs of a grieving heart.

"Blessed are they that mourn," the Bible tells us, "for they shall be comforted." Grief is a solitary act; to mourn means to share with others. When we turn to family and friends following a loss, we are grieving God's way.

This section will offer suggestions for working out difficult relationships by addressing this question: How is God working in our family today? It will also offer tips for creating a healing home and honoring a loved one by reaching out to others in positive, life-affirming ways.

1

GETTING THE WORDS RIGHT

When tragedy strikes,
loving words from a dear friend
heal the wounded heart.

I t's a humbling experience for anyone, but especially a writer, to be at a loss for words. But what do you say to a widow whose husband committed suicide? To a young mother whose three-year-old drowned in a swimming pool? To a child whose father, a policeman, was killed on duty?

In his poem "The Theory and Practice of Rivers," Jim Harrison wrote,

Writers and poets share an
embarrassed moment
when they are sure all
problems will disappear if you get
the language right.

So what are we to do? Stand mutely by the graveside? Avoid contact with the family? Fall back on clichés?

I think back to the days following my son's death, and I remember the words that meant the most to me.

I'm sorry.
I remember when he . . .
I miss him.

Simple words, loving words, words that burrowed into the deepest regions of my heart and stayed there.

Today, take a minute to write a note to that special person whose words touched you during the darkest days of your loss. Too often, we're quick to complain when someone gets the words wrong. Why not take a moment to tell our friends when they get the words right?

"Pleasant words are a honeycomb, sweet to the soul and healing to the bones."

(Proverbs 16:24)

2

HELPING A FAMILY HEAL

Family friction
makes grieving more difficult
for everyone.

The death of a loved one can crumble the very foundation of a family. It's hard to support each other when feelings are raw and everyone's hurting. Healing takes time and patience. Children and teens can be overwhelmed and confused by grief. This can lead to sleeping problems or difficulty concentrating in school. Some children act out anger or guilt in destructive ways.

Parents are often too involved in their own pain to recognize grief in their children, and it helps if a loving relative or friend steps in.

"Live in harmony with one another; be sympathetic, love as broth-ers, be compassionate and humble."

(1 Peter 3:8)

Many problems can be avoided by a few ground rules for family healing. Copy the following rules, filling in the blanks with your loved one's name, and have a family meeting to discuss them. Post the rules in a prominent spot, and refer to them daily.

Rules for Family Healing

- It's okay to talk about feelings, even bad feelings. Talking will help the pain go away.

- Feeling guilty or angry is normal. We all do or say things that we later regret, but none of us is to blame for _____'s death.

- It's okay to cry or feel sad or lonely. Tears help us to heal and feel better. We all miss _____ very much.

- It's okay to laugh. Laughing doesn't mean that we love _____ any less. Laughter is God's way of helping us to connect to each other.

- It's okay to share a memory and mention _____'s name, even if it brings tears, because memories are gifts that are meant to be opened and shared with each other.

- Most important, don't forget to ask for extra hugs whenever you are feeling sad, lonely, or confused (and be prepared to give lots of hugs back).

3

HEALING THE FAMILY, HEALING THE HEART

*"Everyone should be quick to listen, slow to speak and slow to be-
come angry."*

(James 1:19)

Cracks in a building allow sun and air to enter. Broken hearts, shattered spirits, and hurtful relationships can open us up to God's healing presence.

- Opening ourselves to others means accepting their help and comfort. When we say that we're okay when we're not, we create barriers that add to our loneliness.
- Accept the fact that not everyone grieves in the same way or in the same time frame. The family member you think is thoughtless or uncaring might be reacting out of fear or shock.
- Learn to recognize denial in others: some family members protect themselves from grief by overworking or concentrating on things that might seem inappropriate, such as money or estate matters.

- Be aware that you are at your most vulnerable and are probably overly sensitive to what others say or do. Give others—and yourself—a lot of leeway.
- Grief complicated by family problems can be especially draining. Sometimes it helps to take time out. Postpone decisions that do not have to be made right away.
- Plan a family grief evening. Check out a video on grief from your library. Watch the video together and discuss it afterward. Plan a family project day: work on a memorial garden or scrapbook. Cut squares of fabric, and let each family member decorate one with fabric paint in memory of your loved one.
- If decisions must be made, but no agreement can be reached, ask a family friend to arbitrate.
- Ask what's really going on here? A family member who lashes out in anger or hatred is probably acting out of fear.
- If you are not on speaking terms with a family member, write a letter to that person. Don't mail it—just write what you feel. This exercise will help you put things in perspective and identify the source of your anger.
- Seek family counseling, if necessary. If family members won't go with you, go alone.
- Try humor. People connect best when they laugh together. Plan a fun outing, or share a funny family memory. Greet family members wearing a silly disguise. One woman got her sister to speak to her after she sat on the front lawn, waving a white flag.
- Don't become discouraged or hurt if other family members pull away or otherwise seem distant. Turning inward is a normal part of grief.
- Be patient. When friends or family members do or say something hurtful, trust is lost, and rebuilding that trust takes time, but it can be done if hearts are willing.

- Discuss the following question with family members: What do we want our loved one's legacy to be—family strife or family unity?
- Finally, ask yourself this question: How is God working in our family today?

"Confess your sins to each other and pray for each other so that you may be healed."

(James 5:16)

"Hope deferred makes the heart sick . . ."

(Proverbs 13:12)

4

FAMILY PHOTOS

Photos on the fridge
keep you right in the middle
of my busy day.

We have an old family photo of my husband's grandparents and their three children. Dating back to the turn of the century, the photo is the only one that we can find of that particular family, and I think I know why. After the photograph was taken, a son died.

A friend of mine trotted her family to the photographer's studio yearly for their Christmas card photo—until her daughter died in an auto accident six years ago. The family has not been photographed since, nor have they sent out cards.

The first family photo following the death of a loved one can be painful. "I simply can't bring myself to have our picture taken together as a family," one grieving mother confided. "To me, the picture would always be incomplete."

One woman lamented the lack of photographs of her own childhood. "After my brother died, the family unit no longer seemed to exist. We stopped doing things together, and we stopped having our family photo taken."

Sally felt pressured into having her photo taken alone shortly after the death of her husband, when her church decided to put together a photo directory of its members. "I wasn't ready to face my singleness yet, and I resented the church's insensitivity to my feelings."

Posing for a photo can be painful, but it can also send a powerful message to family members that they are valued and still very much a part of a viable and loving family. For the grieving spouse, a photograph can celebrate a newfound personhood.

If it's been longer than a year or two since you or your family have been photographed, it's time. If you're not ready for a professional portrait, plan a picnic and ask someone to photograph the family having fun. Ask a friend to snap a photo of you doing something that you love to do.

You might be surprised to discover that rather than record the emptiness of your life, the camera reveals only the fullness.

"From the fullness of His grace we have all received one blessing after another."

(John 1:16)

5

THE FAMILY THAT PRAYS TOGETHER . . .

*When our family
joins hands around the table,
you are locked inside.*

A family is a tapestry to which each family member contributes to the design. A child is born and weaves his or her own threads throughout the existing pattern. A daughter marries, a grandchild is born, and more threads are added; the pattern changes, becomes more intricate, more complete.

The loss of a loved one can make a family tapestry unravel or fall apart; children, teens, parents, spouses, grandparents, aunts, and uncles can feel at "loose ends" until new roles are established and the threads are rewoven into another design.

What holds things together while the family is regrouping? The answer is found in the old saying "The family that prays together, stays together."

Praying together unites the family in a bond with God. A conference call to God gives the family structure, guidance, and stability. It strengthens each person individually and as a unit; it creates an awareness that the family is not isolated, but rather a vital part of God's plan.

Pray together as a family. Let each member take turns leading prayer. Even the youngest child can learn to praise God, show gratitude, and ask for guidance. Start every family reunion with a prayer, every meal with a blessing. Pray together for the family, for each other, and for friends. Pray together for your loved one.

Any family can be strong during bad times if God is the vital link holding the threads together.

"This, then, is how you should pray: 'Our Father in heaven, hallowed be your name.'"

(Matthew 6:9)

Learn to Respect Each Other's Grieving Styles

Understanding that everyone grieves differently is the first step toward creating harmony in the family. Different grieving styles can be a gift each family member has to give. The husband who has trouble expressing feelings can benefit by listening to his more open wife. The spouse inclined to run away from grief can learn from the partner who faces it head-on. One family member's faith or positive outlook can help lift the spirits of others going through a spiritual crisis. God gave us different grieving styles so that we could help each other heal.

6

A Thousand Ways
to Grieve

Waves of emotion
sink and swell with sudden force,
testing survivors.

I'm an active griever. By *active* I mean that during those first few months following my loss, I devoured every book on grief that I could get my hands on. I poured out my agony in my writing, attended grief seminars, went through photo albums, and searched the Internet for helpful sites. I cried and fumed and spent long hours talking to anyone who would listen.

My husband simply withdrew and grieved in silence. Although we lived in the same house, grieved the same loss, and shared a life together, we were miles apart in our grief.

We all have our own ideas about how to grieve, and we're quick to judge those who don't conform to our way of thinking. When Prince Charles wore a blue suit to Princess Diana's funeral, the press condemned him—until they learned that it was his former wife's favorite.

A friend of mine was criticized for wearing a pair of red strap high-heeled shoes to her husband's funeral, the same shoes that she had worn on the day they met.

If we are to grieve in harmony with those around us, we must give up the notion that grief can be expressed in limited ways. I once thought that grief manifested itself only in tears and depression. But I've since seen what others whose vision is greater than mine have accomplished in the name of grief. Candy Lightner, the founder of Mothers Against Drunk Drivers, is a good example.

Resolve to make peace with someone who grieves in ways that seem odd to you. Try expressing your grief in a new way: write a poem or a song or start a journal. Buy your loved one a gift and send it to someone you know who would love and appreciate the gesture. Wear something outlandish. Buy a bouquet of balloons in your loved one's favorite color. Laugh at something that would make your loved one laugh.

Tears, sadness, and depression are all acceptable ways to show grief. So are blue suits and red shoes.

"There are different kinds of gifts, but the same Spirit."
(1 Corinthians 12:4)

7

THE PRIVATE SIDE OF GRIEF

I turn to the psalms
for pastoral direction
in my time of need.

Grief is an inner journey that requires quiet time alone, away from family pressures and work responsibilities.

It's important to share your grief with friends and family, but there's only so much they can do for you. A friend can hold your hand, but he or she can't carry your burden. A friend can cry with you but only you can do the work of grief. A friend can help you pray, but only you can connect to God.

We live in a society that discourages solitude. Yet solitude is the well from which all art springs. Solitude provides an environment that allows the brain to function at its best; a screening process that allows us to fit together the pieces of our life. Living is an art, and the artist within us thrives on solitude.

Few of us have enough solitude in our lives. Could it be that insomnia is really the soul asking for more time to be alone? To think and to process? Instead of trying to find ways to sleep, perhaps we should simply lie back and enjoy the solitude of the night.

Montaigne wrote, "We must reserve a little back-shop, all our own, entirely free, wherein to establish our true liberty and principal retreat and solitude."

Solitude is perhaps one of the most misunderstood and feared healing processes available to us. Our ancestors took solitude for granted, but we must often fight for the right to be alone with our thoughts. We must fight not only the world at large but also the inner demons that tell us that solitude is akin to loneliness. Nothing could be further from the truth; loneliness is really an inner failure to connect. Solitude connects us with the soul.

Turn off the TV and the radio. Turn off the phones and the chatter. Listen to the quiet, to the music of the soul, to God. Enjoy a solitary walk or a private picnic, or step outside to gaze silently at the stars.

Enter your back-shop daily, and it will take you to wondrous and adventurous places where no one else can go.

"When you pray, go into your room, close the door and pray to your Father, who is unseen."

(Matthew 6:6)

8

WHAT GRIEF WEIGHS

Grief measures itself
by its length of existence
times its depth of pain.

I measure every grief I meet with analytic eyes, Emily Dickinson wrote. "I wonder if it weighs like mine, or has an easier size." We all measure the grief of others against our own. Those who lost a child are convinced that they are the hardest hit. Young widows think that older widows have a less difficult time. Older widows envy the options open to younger widows.

Those whose loved one died without warning view an anticipatory death as a blessing. Those who watched a loved one suffer think that sudden death is less painful, less burdensome—and so it goes.

All of us think that our own loss is greater, our own pain is worse. The imagination simply cannot conceive such pain in others. And so we weigh each other's grief, looking for an easier size that doesn't exist.

"Differing weights and differing measures—the LORD detests them both."

(Proverbs 20:10)

The clock keeps ticking,
but I'm caught in a time warp,
being pulled apart.

9

The Lasting Gift of Time

When I think of you,
the measured moments of time
become infinite.

Time is both friend and enemy to the grieving soul. "How long has it been?" is a question that is almost always answered with utmost accuracy and astonishing detail. One grieving mother told her grief group, "It has been three years, four months, and six and a half minutes."

Another time-related question moved one grieving woman to share her dismay and embarrassment because she wasn't "over it," although it had been three years. "I pretend everything is okay," she said. "And all the time I'm dying inside."

Time can trip us up in countless ways; I recall vividly how much I dreaded the New Year following my son's death. As the minute hand moved ever closer to midnight, I felt as though I were being carried that much farther away from him.

We hear about God's perfect timing, and we want to believe that it's true, but as far as death is concerned, there seems to be no such thing. Either our loved ones die too soon or, in the case of those in pain, not soon enough.

Our grief seems to know no end, and, because we're not going by the book, we feel even more isolated than before.

Although time seems to underscore our failings, it can also mark our growth. One of the lasting gifts of grief is a new appreciation of time's value. One survivor said, "There will be no more time wasted on trivial things, minor disagreements, or irritations. I no longer have time for negative people. Time is too precious."

Today, make time your friend. Instead of counting the minutes separating you from your loved one, count each minute that you feel your loved one's presence.

List the ways that you've come to appreciate time. Perhaps, like many survivors, you now spend more time with family or friends, or in meditation and prayer. Perhaps you've learned to find comfort in the early morning quiet or the stillness that comes with night, and spend more time with God.

Finally, resolve to grieve on your own time schedule. Some of us need extra time to grieve for a variety of reasons. Some deaths are more complicated than others, making grief more difficult. What's important is not how much or little time we grieve, but how *well* we grieve.

> *"For there is a proper time . . . for every matter, though a man's misery weighs heavily upon him."*
>
> (Ecclesiastes 8:6)

Time won't heal grief.

It's what we do with our time that counts. Spiritual wounds require every bit as much attention and care as physical wounds.

Time won't lend a helping hand.

If we were physically wounded, we wouldn't hesitate to seek professional care or to ask our friends for help. Why should emotional pain be treated any differently?

Time won't erase our pain.

Tears will make the pain bearable, but only reconciliation and faith can mend a broken heart.

Time won't make us forget.

If we grieve God's way, we won't forget, but because God encourages forgiveness and compassion, we will remember in more positive and loving ways.

Time won't alleviate the anger.

Anger left to fester turns to bitterness and hatred. We must find positive ways to release our anger, ways that will honor our loved one's memory.

Time won't cure the loneliness.

We must fill our lives with loving friends and family and keep the lines of communication open with God and the church.

Time won't rid us of depression.

Depression is a normal part of grief. The best cure is to embrace life and become involved in meaningful activities.

Healing Ways

"For everyone who asks receives . . ."

(Matthew 7:8)

Why do we say that we're okay when we're not? Why do we say that we're fine when the opposite is true? Why do we put up walls when we most need open doors? How do we get our friends to be more responsive and compassionate?

- Admit that you need help. Say something like:
  "I guess I'm not as brave as I thought I was," or
  "I thought I had everything under control, but the truth is that I'm depressed."
- Ask for help, but be clear and specific:
  "I'm feeling lonely and need to talk. Do you have time to listen?"
  "I need you to hold my hand while I go through my husband's closet."
  "I'm feeling anxious about the holidays. Do you have any suggestions?"

10

HEALING THROUGH DREAMS

Celestial harps
play the accompaniment
to my dreams of you.

Dreams have the power to heal and to restore the soul. Dreams help us to work through problems and put us in touch with our deepest self.

A study of the dreams of pregnant women revealed that women who worked out fears of loss and anxiety in their dreams had the easiest deliveries.

Dreams are guided by the emotions. We dream about what's important to us; we dream about what's closest to the heart. Those of us who are in grief often dream about our loved one. Dreams of a sexual nature are not uncommon following the loss of a spouse. Experts tell us that they are part of the searching process.

Dreams connect us with the past, to the soul, and with God.

God speaks to us through dreams. Numerous reports have been printed of people who were warned in their dreams of an impending illness even before the first symptoms appeared. Writers, inventors, and scientists tell stories about ideas coming to them in dreams.

Dreams allow life and death to coexist; we dream of a loved one, and our weary souls find a respite from grief.

As children, many of us were told to "dream sweet dreams." There was wisdom in those words. Research has shown that dreams affect our moods. Pleasant dreams lead to positive feelings.

So dream a little dream. Think positive thoughts, and recall happy memories before bedtime, and, chances are, your dreams will be sweet.

"I will lie down and sleep in peace, for you alone, O LORD, make me dwell in safety."

(*Psalm 4:8*)

11

THE HEART SEARCHES

*My spirit wanders
on a nomadic search for
an answer to death.*

My neighbor's dog barks and paces the yard whenever its owners leave the house. Such behavior goes back to the time when wild dogs roamed in packs. At the first sign of danger, those early canines howled to summon the pack much like the little pup next door barks to summon his family.

The need to gather our loved ones in times of loneliness or danger is innate. In many cultures, chanting is part of the grieving process, but we all cry out in our own way. Like lonely dogs, we also pace. We walk the floor when we seek answers or a solution to a problem. We wander aimlessly from window to window when a spouse or child is late coming home.

We pace even after the funeral. Intellectually, we know that our loved one is never coming back, but the heart and soul refuses to believe that something so awful could possibly be true. In our anguish, we search for weeks, sometimes even months, after our loved one is gone, crying out our need in a dozen different ways, seeking to find what can't possibly be found, at least not in the way we want. We search until we can no longer deny the truth.

Years ago, the common practice was for a seaman's wife to keep watch for her husband's ship from the bridge, or widow's walk, on her roof. Women often spent days scanning the distant horizon, even when they knew that their husband had been shipwrecked and would never return.

A friend's widowed father kept leaving the house in the middle of the night. He would be gone for hours and refused to talk about where he went. Worried, my friend followed him one night in her car and soon recognized the restaurants, theater, and even the church where her parents spent much of their time together. Her father drove past all of his wife's favorite places, searching for her.

Today, call the *pack* together. Plan a family reunion or outing, and celebrate each other's presence. Stage a treasure hunt. Invite friends over for lunch or dessert, and share memories of the past. Make an effort to touch base with all of the good people in your life.

If you still have the need to pace, cry out, or drive around looking for a loved one, write St. Augustine's words of wisdom on an index card and post it over the kitchen sink: "I sought thee everywhere, my God, but when at last I found Thee, Thou wert within."

"I love those who love me, and those who seek me find me."
                                                          (Proverbs 8:17)

12

THE DARK SIDE OF THE MOON

My moments alone
offer opportunities
to count my blessings.

You have to get out, see people, and do things, they said. "You can't sit home and mope." So I forced myself to go out and do things, although my heart wasn't in them, and I felt miserable.

Eventually, I withdrew and stayed home. In retrospect, this was a good decision on my part. I needed this time alone, away from friends and colleagues, away from people with no understanding of what I was going through. I needed the time to reassess my goals and aspirations, to figure out who I was and how I fit into the big picture.

To reacquaint myself with God, I needed to grieve my son in my own way, without having to meet anyone else's expectations.

Following this period of withdrawal, I gradually came out of my isolation, but I did drop out of many social and professional organizations to join others that better reflect new interests and goals. Dropping out was actually a step forward.

Sometimes we have to do what feels right even if it means going against the counsel and advice of others. Sometimes we need to relegate ourselves to the dark side of the moon.

If you feel as though you're being forced to do something that you're not ready to do, don't do it.

If you think that others are expecting too much of you, say so. If you need more time, take it. The dark side of the moon has a beauty all of its own.

"Wait for the LORD; be strong and take heart and wait for the LORD."
(Psalm 27:14)

13

BAA, BAA BLACK SHEEP . . .

*One day at a time,
mourners pull against sorrow
in a tug of war.*

I was always the black sheep in the family, Barbara told me almost defiantly. Her family couldn't understand why she refused to view her father's body. "I wanted to remember him alive, not dead in a coffin."

Almost every family has a black sheep. Some military families find themselves raising a conscientious objector. A family of overachievers whom I know produced a high school dropout.

When a loved one dies, it's often the family odd ball or the "different drummer" who will say or do something that increases family tension. It's the family black sheep who will probably suggest a break from family tradition, for example, or behave in a way that others deem unconventional or lacking in respect.

Family counselors Gerald Deskin, Ph.D., and Greg Steckler, M.A., wrote in one of their weekly parenting columns for the *Daily News*, "The 'odd' child actually makes the family more whole by pushing it toward balance."

One emotional family was saved from financial woes when their more rational black sheep took over the funeral arrangements. A family of hard-core traditionalists was shocked when a black sheep uncle showed up dressed as a Native American at the memorial service and led the mourners in a prayerful chant. Once the family got over their initial shock, they realized that it was a fitting tribute to the deceased—a man who had spent his life studying Native American culture.

A black sheep represents change, and this is why we sometimes feel threatened. The tension increases if the person challenges our values and beliefs.

To work out these problems takes love and acceptance. You can start by asking yourself these questions: What role does our black sheep play? How does that role bring more balance to the family?

Finally, consider if your "oddball" really is a black sheep—or just another one of the family's treasured assets.

"As I have loved you, so you must love one another."

(John 13:34)

14

THE GIFT OF DEPRESSION

*My sorrow is moored
in a lagoon of mourning,
waiting for high tide.*

I t's my habit as a writer to "set the stage" before beginning a new book. I clean the office, order supplies, and clear my calendar. I put social responsibilities on hold to allow maximum time and energy for my writing. I literally disappear into the book.

In many ways, grieving a loved one requires the same focused attention as writing a book. Depression is God's way of setting the stage and allowing survivors to disappear into grief.

It's important to distinguish between clinical depression that requires medical intervention and healthful depression that makes it possible to grieve fully.

In her book *When Feeling Bad is Good*, Ellen McGrath, Ph.D., describes healthful depression as "based on real life experience" and unhealthful depression as "based on distortion, exaggeration, denial, and delusion."

Normal depression slows us down, pulls us back, and makes us question, seek, and reorganize. More than that, it wraps us in a protective blanket until we regain our inner strength and balance.

In this depressed state, we become more sensitive, more aware, and less willing to take unnecessary chances. Normal depression often brings us closer to God.

Some scientists have even suggested that mild depression is a protective mechanism, keeping us from acting out emotions in an unsafe way.

Healthful depression prevents a grieving widow from selling the family home before she's had time to decide if that's what she wants to do. It's what keeps a new widower from marrying out of loneliness, a grieving parent from lashing out at the world. Depression keeps us close to home, prevents us from making rash decisions, and sets the stage for healing God's way.

"The LORD is close to the brokenhearted and saves those who are crushed in spirit."

(Psalm 34:18)

You're Not Alone!

People in the Bible who suffered from depression include the following:

Abraham	Adam	King Saul
Jonah	Eve	Jeremiah
Job	Cain	David

What to Do for Healthful Depression

- Accept this as an important part of your grief. This dormant period is God's way of preparing you for spiritual and emotional growth.
- Take long, prayerful walks. Listen to all of nature glorify God's name.
- Get at least fifteen minutes of sunlight every day. Fill your lungs with fresh air.
- Write your feelings in a notebook or diary. Write a letter to your loved one. Be honest, and admit your anger or guilt. Write a love letter, an angry letter, a letter of confession or forgiveness. Don't hold back.
- Read the Bible and other inspirational books.
- Treat yourself to the same special care that you would give a family member or friend in need. Exercise, eat healthful foods, and get plenty of rest.
- Listen to music that uplifts and inspires. King Saul called for his musicians during his bouts with depression.
- Spend time exploring the beauty in God's world. Plan a trip to a garden, park, museum, ocean, lake, or mountains. See the face of God.
- Spend time with people who make you feel good. Make a luncheon date with a friend whose faith you admire or who has survived difficult times with grace and wisdom.

Positive thinking
is the hard choice we must make
each day of our lives.

15

SHAPE OF GRIEF

When we're in mourning,
life's cereal bowl turns to
soggy shredded wheat.

Some people grieve in straight lines; others grieve in circles or spirals. Grief can be the shape of a fireball, or as jagged as an iceberg. It can resemble a dark cloud or a deep hole, a high mountain or a lonely desert, a stormy sea or a spring rain. It can be a moving glob, changing shape daily, even hourly, and consuming everything in sight.

In his book *A Grief Observed*, C. S. Lewis wrote about his own grief following the death of his wife. "Am I going in circles, or dare I hope I'm on a spiral? But if a spiral, am I going up or down it?"

What determines the shape of grief? Mainly, the relationship with the deceased. Grief for a loving parent, for example, is generally less traumatic than grief for a rejecting or critical parent. Any hope of resolving problems that plagued a troubled relationship die with the person, and this death of hope intensifies grief.

Circumstances can also influence the shape of grief; a violent or sudden death can lead to complicated grief. The death of a child can cause a more intense grief than the death of an elderly person.

Poor health, depression, divorce, emotional exhaustion, or other losses can have a negative effect on the length and intensity of grief. Death never comes at the "right" time, but prior vulnerability might make it harder to accept the loss.

The shape of grief almost never fits in with society's expectations. Grief is almost always too big, too heavy, and too unwieldy for those around us. We're expected to get over it in six months or less and return to our "old" selves. But the shape of grief refuses to conform to such rigid boundaries.

Draw the shape of your grief on paper. What does it look like and feel like? How much does it weigh? Date your drawing and put it away. In a few months' time, draw your grief again, and compare the two for signs of healing.

Finally, remember that supportive friends and family and, above all, a good relationship with God can turn even the most difficult grief into the shape of love.

> *"Come to me, all you who are weary and burdened, and I will give you rest."*
>
> *(Matthew 11:28)*

16

HEALING THROUGH STRENGTHS

It's from our hard knocks
we gather the strength we need
to persist in life.

Don't be surprised if a fourth *R* is added to your child's curriculum sometime in the near future. Besides reading, 'riting, and 'rithmetic, many schools are now teaching lessons in resilience.

The ability to bounce back has been identified as the most important skill of this millennium. Companies that provide resilience training report that employees recover more quickly following divorce, family illness, or the death of a loved one and take less time from work.

Resilient people believe in someone higher than themselves. They can turn trauma into triumph because they know the source of their strength.

So what makes a person resilient? Connections. Close relationships with others and with God make a person strong. My personal resilience comes from family and faith. My creativity also keeps me strong. Following trauma, I do three things: I pray, I write, and I gather my family around me.

What if you don't know where your strength lies?

Edith Grotberg, Ph.D., head of an international resilience project, breaks it down into three simple steps: "I have (strong relationships, role models, structure); I am (a person who has hope and faith, cares about others, and is proud of myself); I can (communicate, solve problems, seek good relationships)."

Finish the following sentences, and you'll find your source of strength and your road to healing:

I have . . .

I am . . .

I can . . .

"I can do everything through him who gives me strength."

(Philippians 4:13)

When a Relationship Fails

No matter how difficult a relationship is, we all cling to the hope that one day things will be different: the spouse will stop drinking, the son will overcome his drug problem, a parent will finally show approval. Death takes away our last glimmer of hope, and for this we must grieve.

We must also grieve for the relationship that never was, the wasted years, the endless disappointments, the joyless memories, and the bitter tears. We must grieve for the harsh words spoken and the soft words never said and for unexpressed apologies and undeclared love. But most of all we must grieve for the person we never got the chance to be.

17

LETTER TO A FRIEND

Friends structure a pier
high above the angry waves
of the sea of death.

Grief is hard on friendships, but it doesn't have to be. Sometimes all it takes is a little honesty between friends. If we gently and lovingly explain what we need from the relationship during our time of grief, and what we are willing to do in return, we can turn even a lukewarm friendship into something special. Share the following letter with a friend over lunch. You'll both be glad you did.

Dear Friend,

Please be patient with me; I need to grieve in my own way and in my own time. Please don't take away my grief or try to fix my pain. The best thing you can do is listen to me and let me cry on your shoulder. Don't be afraid to cry with me. Your tears will tell me how much you care.

Please forgive me if I seem insensitive to your problems. I feel depleted and drained, like an empty vessel, with nothing left to give. Please let me express my feelings and talk about my memories.

Feel free to share your own stories of my loved one with me. I need to hear them.

Please understand why I must turn a deaf ear to criticism or tired clichés. I can't handle another person telling me that time heals all wounds.

Please don't try to find the "right" words to say to me. There's nothing you can say to take away the hurt. What I need are hugs, not words.

Please don't push me to do things that I'm not ready to do or feel hurt if I seem withdrawn. This is a necessary part of my recovery.

Please don't stop calling me. You might think you're respecting my privacy, but to me it feels like abandonment.

Please don't expect me to be the same as I was before. I've been through a traumatic experience, and I'm a different person.

Please accept me for who I am today.

Pray with me and for me. Should I falter in my own faith, let me lean on yours.

In return for your loving support I promise that, after I've worked through my grief, I will be a more loving, caring, sensitive, and compassionate friend—because I have learned from the best.

Love,
(Your name)

"Greater love has no one than this, that he lay down his life for his friends."

(John 15:13)

"Praise be to God . . . who comforts us in all our troubles, so that we can comfort those in any trouble with the comfort we ourselves have received from God."

(2 Corinthians 1:3–4)

18

FILLING THE VOID

Watching the sunrise
motivates me to escape
my black hole of grief.

One of the assignments that I give students in my creative writing class is to do something new and write about it. One older female student entered a topless contest and won. That's not quite what I had in mind, but I have to admit that her essay was the best. Some people will do anything to get a passing grade.

Some of us will also do anything to fill the void left in the wake of a loved one's death. Some people turn to alcohol or drugs. Others work nonstop. Still others, like the grieving mother, Constance, in Shakespeare's Hamlet, use grief to fill the void:

Grief fills the room up of my absent child, lies in his bed, walks up and down with me; puts on his pretty looks, repeats his words, Remembers me of all his gracious parts, stuffs out his vacant garments with his form; then, have I reason to be fond of grief.

We all have reason to be fond of grief. When grief fills the room, we don't have to deal with the emptiness. When grief fills the bed, we don't have to deal with the loneliness. When grief walks and talks with us, it keeps us from having to face an uncertain future.

Yes, there is a void in our lives, and, yes, it must be filled, but not with relentless grief. We must fill the void with other people, other relationships, other memories, and other dreams. We must fill the void with God.

"My grace is sufficient for you, for my power is made perfect in weakness."

(2 Corinthians 12:9)

Jesus Led a Simple Life

The margins of a day are like bumpers on a car, protecting us from crashing into life. Leaving white space in each day helps prevent burnout and stress by allowing us to keep something of ourselves in reserve. Margins allow time for compassion, love, and prayer—the very essence of friendship.

Jesus led a simple life; consequently, He always had time to listen to those in need.

People living in the fast lane generally ignored my grief or impatiently told me to "get over it." But I was lucky to have a small group of friends whose simple lifestyles left time for matters of the heart and soul.

19

GRIEVING FROM THE HEART

Although I may weep,
goodbye is a painful word
my heart will deny.

I t's tempting to *think* rather than *feel* one's way through grief. Men, more often than women, are inclined to approach grief like a problem to be solved. Real grieving must come from the heart. In her book *A Time to Grieve, Meditations for Healing after the Death of a Loved One,* Carol Staudacher writes, "The brain must follow the heart at a respectful distance."

Washington Irving showed respect for the heart when he wrote, "There is in every heart a spark of heavenly fire which lies dormant in the broad daylight of prosperity, but which kindles up and beams in the dark hour of adversity."

A heart not only kindles and beams but also bursts with pride and jumps with joy. It cries out in loneliness and swells with love. A heart can be pure or worn on a sleeve; it can be open or closed, it can feel light or heavy. A person can be soft or hard-hearted, even heartless.

No emotion is too big or too small to live within the chambers of the heart. Sometimes, we don't even know how much something means to us until we feel tremors inside like an earthquake miles beneath the earth's surface, moving us to tears or joy.

Life unfolds from the inside out, starting with the heart. Sometimes we hear about another's misfortune and *think* that we should do something but don't. At other times, we rush to help someone in distress without thinking because something about the person touched our heart.

We know that we are *thinking* our way through grief when we analyze, criticize, or justify. We know that we are *feeling* our way through grief when we experience sadness, loneliness, or fear.

To feel is to heal.

"For it is with your heart that you believe and are justified . . ."
(Romans 10:10)

Healing Ways

A handsel is a gift given at the beginning of a new venture or New Year as a symbol of good luck. During the War Between the States, a woman often gave her husband or loved one a handkerchief or scarf to tuck in his shirt, close to his heart, before he rode off to battle.

Some families give each other handsels as they begin the journey of grief. After losing her husband, one woman gave miniature boats to her three teenage sons to symbolize the need for the family to "row" together.

Another family passed out little crosses, symbols of faith and hope, at the funeral of a beloved grandfather.

Handsels come in all shapes and sizes—but they can symbolize the best that the human spirit has to offer: hope, faith, courage, and love.

20

IF ONLY . . .

Honest emotions
gently bathe an aching heart,
calming its torment.

Bob blames himself for his brother's suicide. "If only I had known how deep his depression was."

Diane blames herself for her mother's death. "If only I had made her go to the doctor sooner."

If only I had . . .
If only I'd said . . .
If only I'd known . . .

Grief almost always comes with its own brand of guilt. Sometimes guilt is warranted; we have all said and done things that we've regretted. But even the most minor, normal, every day offenses can turn into heart-wrenching guilt in the face of death.

Sometimes it's a failure to say or do something that makes us feel guilty.

In *Healing After the Suicide of a Loved One*, authors Ann Smolin, C.S.W., and John Guinan, Ph.D., write the following comforting words: "Whatever course you fault yourself for not having taken, there is someone else blaming himself for having taken the same course."

Guilt can be self-destructive and lock us into the past, but it can also be a stepping stone to healing.

Guilt forces us to reassess beliefs and refine our sense of justice. In learning to forgive ourselves, we learn to forgive others.

If you're struggling with guilt, determine what lessons can be learned from your past mistakes.

Real healing comes when we can turn the "if onlys" and the "I should haves" of the past into the "I wills" of the future.

"Godly sorrow brings repentance that leads to salvation and leaves no regret . . ."

(2 Corinthians 7:10)

21

THE JOYS OF SELFHOOD

I'm slowly learning
how to accept each new day
and live each minute.

Mary claims she waited for her deceased husband to fix the car. "The car sat on the side of the street for a month, where it had broken down, before I finally got it into my head, I had to call the tow truck myself."

Linda admits to letting everyone do for her the first year after her husband died. "His brothers and my son made me feel helpless. Finally, I said, 'Enough, already.' I was going to do for myself, even if it meant doing it wrong."

In her book *Widow to Widow*, Genevieve Davis Ginsburg writes, "We are all winners when we are self-reliant and satisfied with ourselves—when selfhood takes the place of widowhood."

A widowed friend of mine tiled her bathroom after taking a course at a local home-improvement store. Another widow learned to refinish furniture by watching a do-it-yourself video. A widower with two children took cooking lessons. One woman learned to put up dry wall by volunteering to build houses for the Habitat for Humanity project.

Selfhood means you've moved beyond being someone's child, spouse, or parent, and discovered and accepted your own unique self.

God has blessed each of us with strengths that we don't even know we possess until we need them. He has instilled within us the necessary tools to heal and be healed.

Find your own feet by learning and doing; move your thinking beyond widowhood, childlessness, or the status of orphan, and you'll turn grief into a whole new selfhood.

"All things are possible with God."

(Mark 10:27)

Healing Ways

When Jesus said, "I will make you fishers of men," He was talking about going out and spreading God's Word. But he was also talking about the importance of spreading a safety net of our own by filling our lives with positive people. By surrounding ourselves with a loving church family and friends who share our faith, we create a community of healing.

22

STARS SHINE IN DARKNESS

In a moonless phase,
when the sky turns ebony,
stars twinkle brighter.

Grief is the darkest of nights, the blackest of blacks. We feel numbed, shocked, empty. The world as we knew it has ended.

Slowly, the clouds move, and we suddenly become aware of the "stars" in our life. One star that shone brightly for me was my friend Betty, whose early-morning calls boosted me during my darkest days. She never failed to make me smile through the tears.

After Kimberly's son was killed by a drunk driver, her star was a young mother, who'd lost her daughter the same way. "She was the north star that kept me on course when all I wanted to do was lay down and die."

Harriet's star was her church. "Following the death of my husband, the people were wonderful and made certain I wasn't alone during the holidays."

Sometimes the "stars" that shine brightest in our grief are the ones we didn't even know existed. Vicky said, "My friends pretty much let me down, but a woman I barely knew made a special memorial candle for my son and invited me to her church, where I found a new home."

Some people *are* stars; other people *lead* us to stars. Greg's daughter practically dragged him to a widow/widower grief group, and it changed his life. "I met Kate, who was further along in her grief than me, and she refused to let me feel sorry for myself. She wasn't just a shining star; she was a super star. That was five years ago, and we just celebrated our second wedding anniversary."

Leading a grief-stricken person to a star can be tricky. Nelly Sachs of Calvary Hospital wrote, "Show us your sun, but gradually. Lead us from star to star, step by step. Be gentle when you teach us to live again."

Declare today to be "show appreciation to the 'stars' in your life" day. Roll out the red carpet, and take a "star" to lunch. Send a card or flowers in appreciation. Make one of your "star's" wishes come true.

Finally, if you know someone who is lost in the night, shine a light in the darkness, lead them to a star, and then, ever so gently, show them the sun.

"When they saw the star, they were overjoyed."

(Matthew 2:10)

23

FRIENDS WHO GRIEVE TOGETHER . . .

Compassionate friends
know the art of listening
with their ears and heart.

Modern society is tough on friendships. People once depended on friends for their very existence. They got together to raise barns and to work the farm, perhaps even to deliver a baby. Because times were tough, no one could afford the luxury of a fair-weather friend.

Friends are still part of our lives today but in a very different way. Mostly, we get together to play. We laugh together but seldom cry together. We do fun things such as go to the movies or party, but seldom are we called upon to help out in a life-or-death situation.

Instead of bonding because of what we've been through together, we bond because of the roles we play. Married couples make friends with other married couples, and when one dies, it leaves the surviving partner feeling like a fifth wheel. Childless parents might no longer feel comfortable around other parents. Seldom does a modern friendship have a chance to bond in a way that will carry it through the bad times.

The death of a loved one is a testing ground for friends. Friendships based on fun times are too shallow to survive the strains of grief. It's not unusual for the bereaved to drop all, if not most, of their old friends following the death of a loved one. Grief can break up friendships, but it can also bring people together. Coworkers, for example, often grow closer following the death of a colleague.

Sometimes, we find friends in unexpected places. The person we hardly know admits to a similar loss, and suddenly we connect.

Through the revealing eyes of grief, friendships can grow closer or fall apart. In times of grief, we learn who our *real* friends are, and that discovery is a blessing. Fair-weather friends are a dime a dozen, but the *real* friend is a treasure to be cherished.

> *"Dear friends, let us love one another, for love comes from God."*
> (1 John 4:7)

Healing Ways

Sometimes we have such high expectations of the people we care about that it's impossible for anyone to live up to them. Here's the reality:

No friend can know how you feel—only God can.
No friend can meet *all* of your needs—only God can.
No friend can bear your burden for you—only God can.
No friend can read your mind—only God can.
No friend can heal your pain—only God can.

24

THE HEALING
MARRIAGE

*Now I realize
how closely interwoven
two lives can become.*

T he prevailing dream is to marry for love, but, regardless of whether we know it, we almost always marry for purposes of healing.

"He listens to me," my daughter told us about the man she was about to marry, and her father and I felt immensely relieved. Good listening skills are one of the most important steps toward communication, but it's also a key ingredient for a healing marriage.

"He makes me feel safe," a friend, a former abused woman, told me on the eve of her second marriage. Another friend insists that she fell in love with her husband because he made her laugh. Laughter and security are both great healers.

Loving and being loved is, in itself, healing, too, but there's always some underlying reason why two people fall in love, some inner need that must be met before we choose a life partner.

When the healing sanctity of marriage is rocked by a death in the family, especially the death of a child, it only adds to the feeling of isolation and loss. When both partners need to heal, neither can adequately comfort the other.

At such times, a simple apology can help clear the air. "I'm sorry I've pushed you away" or" "I'm sorry that my pain has made me insensitive" are good starters.

Ask for time out. Say something like, "I know I'm not very giving right now, but I need more time."

Joining a couples' grief support group can help parents work through their grief and strengthen a marriage.

Talk to a marriage or grief counselor. Talk to your pastor or priest. Pray together, and take turns reading the Bible aloud.

Sometimes it helps to have a common task or job to do. Work together on a memorial project. Some couples have started a foundation or scholarship program in honor of a lost child. Others have created a memorial garden or volunteered time at a hospital. One couple I know became certified grief counselors after losing parents on both sides. Reaching out to others will help you heal both individually and as a couple.

"The LORD God said, 'It is not good for the man to be alone. I will make a helper suitable for him.'"

(Genesis 2:18)

25

A RIVER RUNS THROUGH IT

*A bubbling brook flows
over the rocks in its path,
singing all the way.*

Grief has a way of damming up inside and cutting us off from everything and everyone we care about until we can no longer receive or give joy. We block out the good in our lives and focus solely on the bad. We stop reaching out to others, and eventually they stop reaching out to us. Once the river of humanity stops flowing through our lives, we stagnate in depression.

How do we get things flowing again? It's not easy because it requires that we give up something, maybe even a part of ourselves. Having already suffered a tremendous loss, who can blame us for not wanting to give up something more?

Yet, giving up and giving back is the first step to unblocking the dam keeping us from the good things in life. For me, this meant turning my son's bedroom into a guestroom. It was a painful decision, but the room was tearing me apart. Sometimes I would leave the door ajar, trying to pretend that everything was okay. At other times, I slammed the door shut, unable to stand the empty silence.

Although it was difficult to strip the walls and furnishings from the room and start afresh, it was a necessary part of the healing process. Our newly decorated guestroom has since provided comfort to a young mother nursing a sick son, sheltered a troubled friend, and nurtured various family members in need of special care. The flow of humanity is a much more fitting tribute to my son than an empty room because he loved people and would have been the first to give up his room to a friend in need.

Where are the dams in your life? What are you holding on to? Is it the pain? The loneliness? Are you holding on to your loved one's possessions? To old grudges? Let go of the anger and bitterness; let the river of goodness and hope flow.

"A generous man will himself be blessed, for he shares his food with the poor."

(*Proverbs 22:9*)

26

THE ART OF COURAGE

While grieving God's way,
we seek and share compassion
with understanding.

Following the death of her brother, my daughter suffered such a deep depression that although she was receiving grief therapy, she literally could not get up in the morning. For weeks, I called her daily and walked her through the process. "Come on now. Sit up. That's the way. Now put your feet on the floor. That's a girl. Now . . ." Step by step, I "walked" her to the shower.

Grief, stripped down to the basic bones, could be described as the loss of courage. It takes courage to do even the most mundane tasks. Getting out of bed takes courage because it requires a willingness to face life.

Courage is the driving force behind every action. Without courage, driving a car, shopping for groceries, or even making a phone call can seem daunting.

When we lose a loved one, we lose courage, and that's why we find it so hard to get through the day. It takes courage to be alone or to face what seems like a bleak future. It takes courage to admit to anger or a lack of faith. It takes courage to change, to grow, to put together a broken heart, to heal.

How do we gain the courage necessary to get on with our lives? Monica Lehner Kahn wrote, "Condolence is the art of giving courage." If you need to do something but can't, ask a special someone for help. A friend can give you courage by . . . holding your hand while you make a dreaded phone call, . . . staying with you while you sort through a loved one's belongings, . . . sitting with you during worship, . . . accompanying you to a grief counselor or grief meeting, . . . helping you look for a new place to live, or . . . praying with and for you.

I gave my daughter courage until such time as she was able to regain her own. Today, she is the happy mother of two preschoolers, and that is about as courageous as one can get!

"May (God the Father) encourage your hearts and strengthen you in every good deed and word."

(2 Thessalonians 2:17)

27

SACRED MOMENTS

Memories can choose
only the happy moments
to keep forever.

For years, I played bridge every Friday afternoon with three women friends. We called this our weekly "whine-down." We generally played at Mary's house because, unlike the rest of us, she didn't have teens at home, and her house was blissfully quiet.

Mary was known for her beautiful garden, and that's where we found her each week, awaiting our arrival. Mary always talked about the importance of pinching off wilted blooms to keep them from stealing valuable nutrients from new blossoms.

It's been more than ten years since Mary's death, but I never fail to think of her as I walk around my garden snipping off dead blooms. I've come to think of such moments as sacred.

Sacred moments have a way of revealing themselves in unexpected ways. The simple act of lighting a candle never fails to bring back memories of a deceased friend who filled her house with them. Even tucking a quilt over a sleeping child brings warm memories of a quilting friend whose life was cut short by cancer.

Peeling an orange, walking in the rain, seeing a rainbow, and hearing a certain song are just a few of the everyday occurrences that can bring back happy memories of friends and relatives whom we have lost through the years.

Make today a day of sacred moments. Light a candle in honor of some special someone in your life. Treat yourself to a loved one's favorite dessert. Buy a balloon in memory of someone who loved them. Celebrate your loved one's gift of generosity by leaving a dollar for a child to find. Say a prayer of thanksgiving for the special people who have crossed your path.

The little details of life become sacred moments when they help us to remember and honor our loved ones with a smile!

"Do not grieve, for the joy of the LORD is your strength."
(Nehemiah 8:10)

Healing Ways

Women typically find comfort in sharing their feelings with others and tend to find grief groups helpful. Men, most often, find comfort in doing. One woman managed to get her husband to discuss the loss of their son during a weekend fishing trip.

"'Go,' said Jesus, your faith has healed you.'"

(Mark 10:52)

PART FOUR

Healing the Grieving Spirit

Society's Way:
Time heals.

God's Way:
Faith heals.

Introduction to Part 4

When grieving God's way,
peace of mind is the reward
we receive for faith.

We sink into a dark cave. Hope and joy are distant memories. The very foundation of our faith collapses, and nothing seems to exist beyond the dark walls. We cry out to God, but our cries go unanswered. We question His wisdom and purpose. This is how the spirit grieves.

Fortunately, God doesn't hold our loss of faith against us; He forgives us for our doubts and anger and sometimes even rewards us with a stronger faith. This is the wonder of God's amazing grace.

The spirit heals when life becomes meaningful again, and we face the future with hope, courage, and a more lasting and mature faith.

1

THE HEALING POWER OF PRAYER

*My faith is a kite
that carries me to the heights
where I talk to God.*

Recently, I tried to contact the president of a small corporation. I spent a good fifteen minutes trying to work my way through the voicemail, pressing one number after another, until I finally gave up in frustration.

Think of how awful it would be if God had voicemail. What if every time we wanted to talk to Him, we had to push 1 for needs, 2 for wants, and 3 for forgiveness?

Each of us has a direct line to God available to us twenty-four hours a day, seven days a week. If, for some reason, we can't reach Him, the problem is always on our side.

Prayer is essential to our well-being, to our souls, to our spiritual growth. Prayer forces us to put our thoughts in order and our feelings into words. Prayer helps us to focus on something outside of self; it reminds us that someone else is in charge.

God commands us to praise Him, not for Himself, because He has no need for praise and adulation, but for our own spiritual fulfillment. When we praise and show gratitude to God, we become more godlike. In glorifying God, life becomes more glorious.

The most important thing to remember about prayer is that it is a dialogue between *two* people. God listens to us and expects us to listen to Him in return. God doesn't have voicemail—and where He is concerned, neither should we.

"Pray continually."

(*1 Thessalonians 5:17*)

Healing God's Way through Prayer

Make prayer a part of your daily life. Spend time each morning in prayer—even if you feel disconnected from God. Talk to God each afternoon. Share a thought with Him over lunch; confess a fear to Him before dinner. Praise Him when you're in the car or each time you enter your home. Invite God to go for a walk with you; make Him part of your nightly ritual. Instead of tossing and turning at night, talk to God. Let Him into your anguished heart; let Him soothe your grieving soul.

2

PRAYING TO A SILENT GOD

When grieving God's way,
prayer provides the solace
that heals wounded souls.

God, why didn't you answer my prayers? I demanded in the early days of my grief. "How could you do this to me? You're nothing but a fraud!"

The more I ranted, the more silence I endured. It was like talking to a block wall. Finally, I gave up talking to God altogether.

During this time, my daughter called to talk over a personal problem. After discussing it at length, she stopped and asked, "Mom, are you there?" Her question startled me. Of course I was there, listening to her every word.

It suddenly occurred to me that it wasn't an *absent* God whom I had encountered in my prayers but a *silent* God, a *listening* God.

It would have done Him no good to have spoken to me. I wouldn't have heard Him if He had. That's how angry, how enraged, and how absolutely lost in my grief I was.

Humbled, I fell on my knees for the first time in months, and, this time, I was ready to listen to what God had to say.

If you haven't yet expressed your anger at God, do so. God might not say anything at first, but He *will* listen—and later, when the time is right—He *will* answer.

> *"The LORD has heard my cry for mercy; the LORD accepts my prayer."*
> *(Psalm 6:9)*

To believe while not understanding is a desirable goal yet believing without thinking can leave us stunted.

Used by permission of
Bereavement *magazine*
1-888-604-4673 (HOPE)

3

ALL IN GOD'S TIME

Time heals so slowly,
a broken heart may believe
there's no hope for it.

Research continues to shed new light on the grieving process, but the tendency is still to measure the healing of the human spirit in *chronos* time. *Chronos* time is measured with watches and calendars. Because it's easy to understand, we try to fit everything, even emotions, into the little spaces on a calendar.

But matters of the heart and soul can never be measured so neatly. Love and grief can be measured by only what the Greeks called *kairos* time. *Kairos* is the *right* time, or timing; it's when everything comes together, creating a moment of magic, if you will, a moment of the greatest potential.

When you study biology and learn about the conditions necessary for conception, you realize what a miracle it is that any one of us is here. Conception is truly a *kairos* moment.

In her book *Walking on Water: Reflections on Faith and Art*, Madeleine L'Engle calls *kairos real time, God's time.* She writes,

"The artist at work is in *kairos*. The child at play, totally thrown outside himself in the game, be it building a sand castle or making a daisy chain, is in *kairos*. In *kairos*, we become what we are called to be as human beings, co-creators of God, touching on the wonder of creation."

Forget about the calendar; forget about the clock. Make a sign that reads *Following God's Time,* and hang it in a prominent spot.

So how long does it take to grieve? As long as it takes God to heal.

"Trust in him at all times . . ."

(Psalm 62:8)

Grief can't be rushed. It must unfold with the same exquisite timing as a rose, and left to bloom until the colors fade, and the petals fall away of their own accord.

4

FINDING NEW MEANING IN GOD'S WORD

God's favorite game
seems to be hide-and-go-seek,
so I keep searching.

L osing a loved one sets us apart. It opens our hearts and minds
in ways we never imagined, and we begin to understand
things that previously escaped our attention. Even familiar
Scriptures take on a whole new meaning when we lose a loved one.

One Scripture that took on new meaning for me personally is
"Jesus wept." This is the shortest verse in the Bible and perhaps
even the most powerful. Jesus wept although He was about to res-
urrect His friend Lazarus. In giving in to this very human emotion, Jesus demonstrated that although we might believe in
everlasting life and know that our loved ones are in a better place,
it's okay to grieve. Jesus wept, and so should we.

Read your favorite Scriptures, and let God's previously hidden
messages comfort you in your grief.

"As for God, his way is perfect; the word of the LORD is flawless."
(Psalm 18:30)

Sunshine lifts the dew
as gently as loving words
raise broken spirits

5

OUR FAITH IS TESTED

My anger at God
frightens me when it rages,
yet it eases pain.

Many of us have never taken the time to work on our spiritual lives. We took a leap of faith as children and never bothered to examine our beliefs or allow our devotion to God to go much beyond an elementary level.

Then one day we lose someone we love. Although we never before questioned the wisdom or even the existence of God, we suddenly find ourselves questioning it now. Our faith deserts us in our greatest need.

Still, we have to wonder if any of us can put our trust in a faith that has not been tested. Even C. S Lewis, a brilliant scholar and Christian essayist, pondered this question following the death of his wife. In *A Grief Observed*, he wrote, "You never know how much you really believe anything until its truth or falsehood becomes a matter of life and death to you. It is easy to say you believe a rope to be strong and sound as long as you are merely using it to cord a box. But suppose you had to hang by that rope over a precipice."

Does our faith really desert us, or is it simply our childish beliefs that we lose? Is our anger at God and the questioning of His existence a necessary step toward gaining a deeper, more mature faith?

If you find your own faith floundering or suddenly start questioning the existence of God, don't despair. Doubting one's belief system is often the seed that leads to the lasting gift of a deeper, more mature faith.

Find an acorn and slip it into your pocket as a reminder that all great things start from little seeds. Find a beautiful spot in the garden or park where you feel close to God. Before faith can grow, we must appreciate our gifts and understand our limitations. So begin by giving a prayer of thanksgiving. If the words won't come, then simply repeat these words: *Thank you, God. Thank you for this chance to renew my faith.*

"... *the LORD tests the heart.*"

(*Proverbs 17:3*)

It's hard to be angry at a stranger. If you're angry with God, it means you have an on-going relationship with Him.

6

FINDING YOUR WAY
BACK TO GOD

"My God, my God, why have you forsaken me?"

(Mark 15:34)

J esus died for our sins on a cross. His greatest pain, however, was not the physical suffering; it was the pain caused by the heavy burden that He carried because these sins separated Him from God the Father.

Those of us whose faith is shaken following the loss of a loved one can relate to the anguish, the crying out for God, the hopelessness. But just as Jesus opened the gates of heaven, so must we find our way back to God.

- **Keep your heart and soul open to God.** The Bible tells us that faith is the assurance of things hoped for, the conviction of things not seen. Faith, then, is described as hope, assurance, and conviction. Conviction comes with knowledge, and the only way we can understand the masterful plan that God has for our life is to open heart and soul to God's Word.

- **Admit your anger at God.** In his book *Sit Down, God . . . I'm Angry*, R. F. Smith Jr. writes, "Admitting anger, especially at God, is not heresy. It is a healing step; it is trust in action, the belief that God not only understands, but cares."
- **Don't do it alone.** The loss of a loved one is more than anyone can handle alone. Call a friend whose faith you admire, or make an appointment to see a trusted priest, pastor, or rabbi to ask for direction and prayer.
- **Read the Bible.** The Bible is a book made to order for the grieving heart and the searching soul. The truths contained within its pages are revealed slowly and only as we need them. Sometimes it's necessary to reach a certain spiritual level before we can work out the intricate lessons for ourselves, and sometimes this requires the wisdom that comes with grief.
- **Read books by others who are struggling with their faith.** Such books can inspire us and provide models for us to follow. In *A Grief Observed*, C. S. Lewis writes about his struggles with faith following the loss of his wife. *Making Loss Matter: Creating Meaning in Difficult Times* by Rabbi David Wolpe is a beautiful, inspirational book that touches on questions we all ask about life, death, faith, and hope following the death of a loved one.
- **Act faithful.** Action precedes feelings. It's almost impossible to feel faithful to God without first *acting* faithful. If reading the Bible and praying are not part of your daily life, it will be almost impossible to nurture the kind of faith that will carry you through trial and tribulation. Faith, like everything else, follows action.

The Bible is filled with universal truths that speak to the masses and are custom-made for the individual.

"When I was a child, I talked like a child, I thought like a child.
When I became a man I put childish ways behind me."

(1 Corinthians 13:11)

7

WHY DID GOD LET THIS HAPPEN?

I move in circles,
like a goldfish in a bowl,
searching for answers.

W hy? I asked my pastor during the days of my deepest and darkest despair. "Why did someone so young have to die?"

His reply was comforting because he didn't give me a pat answer. He told me that our lives are a tapestry, and we see only the working side: the knots where we've changed directions, the loose threads of unfinished work, the mistakes and false starts, and the places where we've lost our way. He went on to say that after we die, we'll have a much clearer picture, and if we've lived our lives to the best of our ability, we will have created a tapestry that will make us proud.

In his book *Once Upon A Number: The Hidden Mathematical Logic of Stories*, John Allen Paulos writes "that the brain's complexity, including its factual knowledge, associations, and reasoning ability, is necessarily limited." No one knows for sure how many bits make up the brain, but it's been estimated that it's something like three billion. Paulos insists that the "existence of the number is more important than its value."

Paulos explains that we will never understand some things because our brains don't have enough bits. He suggests that the scientific and religious approaches to finding a theory for everything is based on "naïve assumptions that such a theory can be found and that its complexity will be sufficiently limited to be understood by us."

In our youth, we seek answers for everything. Eventually, we come to accept the idea that the really important questions involving life and the universe don't necessarily have answers—at least not answers that our brains can understand.

None of us knows why our loved one had to die, and I'm not even sure we should know. Isn't it more comforting to think that the answer is so complex and so profound as to be outside our realm of understanding?

We'll never know all of the answers, but the important thing is to keep tying those knots on the back of our tapestries, yes, even while we grieve. One day, we might even find that we've created a masterpiece.

"God's voice thunders in marvelous ways; he does great things beyond our understanding."

(Job 37:5)

Declare Today "Celebrate the Mysteries of Life Day"

Study a star-studded sky, find a baby to hug, stare at a tree, watch the beginning of young love, and listen to children at play.

Seek out a bird taking flight, an apple falling to the ground, a rose beginning to bloom. Follow a butterfly around the garden, or gaze upon a spider spinning its web. Listen to your heartbeat. Praise God for the mysteries of the universe.

God is always there
despite our unsuccessful
attempts to reach Him.

8

BACK TO BASICS

The secret of life
is only learned as we lose
someone close to us.

For me, the last chapter of a book is the hardest to write. In the early days of my career, I spent days rewriting a problematic ending, never quite getting it right. Eventually, I learned that if the end of the story doesn't work, it's the first chapter that's at fault.

Going back to the beginning is a good way to solve many of life's problems. A return to one's roots, for example, might help a person regain a sense of self-worth or purpose. A walk down memory lane can help troubled couples remember why they fell in love in the first place. A spiritual crisis can often be resolved if we go back to the core of our faith.

"Why did God let this happen?" we might ask, following the death of a loved one. "Why didn't He answer my prayers? How could something so awful be God's will?"

These questions might best be answered with more questions: "Is my God too small? Is my vision too limited? Is my faith too narrow?"

A *yes* to any or all of these questions places the burden on us. It means that we have work to do. We must go back to the first "chapter" of our faith and broaden our definition of God. We must struggle to understand if not the intent of God's will at least the scope of it. We must learn to accept both God's sovereignty and man's freedom of choice. Somewhere between these two extremes, we'll find peace.

Write a letter to God, and don't mince words. God is a loving parent who understands and accepts our spiritual struggles. List the questions you have; write out the *whys* and the *how-could-yous*. Then read in the Bible about other people's struggles and God's answers to them.

Broadening your vision of God is the first step toward developing a stronger, more healing faith.

> *"In the beginning was the Word, and the Word was with God, and the Word was God."*
>
> (John 1:1)

9

THE WHO'S AND
WHAT'S

*My philosophy
for the future will be to
enjoy each moment.*

If you're a Winnie-the-Pooh fan, you know that sometimes he sits around wondering *who* is *what* and *what* is *who*. The *who's* and *what's* following the loss of a loved one sound something like this: Who am I? Whom do I trust? In what do I believe? What is the meaning of life? As unsettling as these questions might be, they are a necessary part of forming a philosophy of life.

My personal philosophy is pretty basic; our five-year-old complains about some imagined injustice, and I tell him that "life's not fair" or "that's the way the cookie crumbles." A personal or career set-back sends me scurrying around to *make* "lemonade out of lemons."

The signs in my home speak to the *who* and *what* questions that I've asked myself over time. One, a picture of Winston Churchill, reminds me, "Never give up." A sign over my sink reads, "Life takes a toll, bring change." This one is posted next to my computer: "A dead-end is a great place to make a U-turn." On those days when I'm tempted to regret my past, there's this: "It's never too late for a happy childhood."

When I'm in a self-critical mood, the sign that reads "Be patient, God's not finished with me yet" puts me in a more positive frame of mind.

During the darkest days of my grief, I found comfort in the Scripture hanging on the bathroom mirror: "For God so loved the world . . ."

Words of wisdom, words to live by, words that speak to the *who's* and the *what's* of my life.

In his book *Happiness is a Serious Problem*, author and radio host Dennis Prager writes, "Without a philosophy of life, we do not know how to react to what life deals us. . . . Without being able to place events into perspective—which comes from having a philosophy of life—we are at the mercy of events. Our ship has no destination and no compass."

Even if we have a compass, sometimes it points in the wrong direction; our philosophy is sound for the little annoyances of everyday life, but it falls short when we're dealing with real tragedies. Keep your philosophical compass in good working order; review the *who's* and the *what's* of your life.

A philosophy of life doesn't ensure smooth sailing ahead, but it does improve navigation skills. So decorate your home and office with those wise little sayings that keep you on track. Meanwhile, *never give up; if life gives you lemons, make lemonade*—and never forget that *a dead-end is a great place to make a U-turn*. Above all else, put your trust in the Lord.

"The LORD is my strength and my shield; my heart trusts in him, and I am helped."

(Psalm 28:7)

10

GRIEF IN DISGUISE

In turtle fashion,
I get the urge to withdraw
'neath my shell of grief.

The Bible tells the story of two women who were fighting over the same child. When King Solomon ordered the child to be cut in two, one woman—the real mother—offered to give up her son rather than let him die. The other woman offered no such plea; she made it perfectly clear that if she couldn't have the boy, no one should have him.

How could anyone be that cold and uncaring? How could anyone stand by and allow an innocent child to be killed?

Grief comes in many disguises and one of them is denial. That woman had lost her own baby, but instead of grieving her loss, she stole another woman's child. She was clearly in denial when she claimed the other child as her own.

It's hard to imagine how a woman who loved a child so much that she couldn't bare to accept its death would allow another child to be cut in two. But unresolved grief does strange things to a person; it can turn a heart into stone and stain a soul black.

Described as a harlot, the grieving mother probably had no friends or family, no place to share her grief, and no visible means of expressing her pain. She was angry and filled with envy and hatred. Why did her child die and another child live? She was clearly striking out at the world.

Unresolved grief takes on many guises. It can dress up like anger or wear the mask of bitterness. Unresolved grief lurks in the overachiever who is working sixteen hours a day, lingers in the homeless person who can't face life, and hides in the fun-loving clown who is desperate to fill the world with laughter.

Grief ignored can disguise itself as hatred and walk into a crowded building behind a blazing gun. It can dress up as road rage or lash out in a bar brawl. Unexpressed grief can be the backbone of depression and the monster behind alcohol, drug abuse, and even suicide.

Unresolved grief won't disappear or leave us alone. It is always there, waiting to be unmasked. God instilled within us the need to grieve; it's a need that must not, cannot, and should not be ignored.

"For whatever is hidden is meant to be disclosed, and whatever is concealed is meant to be brought out into the open."

(Mark 4:22)

11

TO HOPE AGAIN

Nature's spring palette
softly covers winter's gloom
with new life and hope.

Nothing is worse than a life without hope. Hope is the beacon that shines into the future; hope is confidence that God is leading the way.

Hope keeps us going when things look the darkest, keeps us plugging away when the last door seems to be shut tight. "Hope," Emily Dickinson wrote, "is the thing with feathers that perches in the soul."

That thing with feathers helps us to fly, to soar upward to a higher self, to keep our sights on land ahead. Healing requires hope, and we must medicate ourselves with hope daily or, if necessary, even hourly.

How do we regain hope when someone we love dies? Start by connecting to things that go beyond the moment. Smile at a baby, or play with a puppy. Plant a tree, or plan a special trip or family gathering. Fill a flowerbox with daffodils, the flower of hope. Spend time with hopeful people, people who have goals and dreams, people whose faith you admire. Scatter feathers of hope wherever you go.

"May the God of hope fill you with all joy and peace as you trust in him . . ."

(Romans 15:13)

12

GOD THE BEACON

God is the beacon
that guides my floundering ship
through the sea of grief.

Some people's faith remains constant even in their deepest grief; others discover that their faith is but a candle that can be blown out with the slightest breeze.

The rest of us fall somewhere in between; it takes the gale-like winds of death to extinguish *our* candles. Finding ourselves in darkness, we rail against God, the church, the doctors, our families, and anyone who dares to suggest that the terrible loss of our loved one is God's will.

In our anguish, we feel cheated and angry, and more than anything, alone. We ask why God has abandoned us, and it never occurs to us that we are the ones who abandoned Him.

Grief can be the bridge that moves you from the passive faith of youth to a more active, life-affirming faith that can take you to heights of awareness and understanding that you never thought possible. Grieving God's way can help you turn your burned-out candle into an everlasting beacon.

"Your word is a lamp to my feet and a light for my path."

(Psalm 119:105)

When I'm feeling blue,
God's words of encouragement
echo in my head.

13

GIFTS OF NATURE

Weeping willow trees
represent nature's mourning
with grace and beauty.

When we want to feel close to God, many of us instinctively turn to nature. If God is everywhere, why do we feel closer to Him in the woods, mountains, or even a garden than anywhere else? The answer is simple: the nature of God doesn't change with the environment—we do.

The city often makes us feel rushed and stressed. Nature slows us down and makes us more receptive, more open, and more aware. In the city, we tend to walk head down, eyes focused ahead. In nature, we lift our eyes upward to the treetops, to mountains and sky, into the face of God.

In the city, our thoughts are dictated by outside forces. Nature provides a playground for the soul; our spirits soar, and our thoughts are free to roam.

Little softness exists in the city; it's mostly concrete and steel and has fewer places to heal. Nature is as soft as a mother's loving arms, filled with signs of healing.

In the city, we shout to be heard, and seldom do we hear others praise God. In the great outdoors, even our deepest and most profound thoughts can be spoken in silence, and the very wind utters His name.

Naturalist John Muir was a great believer in the healing powers of nature. In *John of the Mountains,* he wrote, "Come to the wood, for here is rest."

Open your heart and soul to nature's healing force; let your spirit fly. Listen to all of nature praise His name.

"But Jesus often withdrew to lonely places and prayed."
Luke 5:16

Healing Ways

"Come, let us go up to the mountain of the LORD . . ."
(Micah 4:2)

Mountains are found throughout the Bible. Moses received the Ten Commandments on Mount Sinai. Jesus traveled up a mountain when He wanted to be alone with God. This climbing of mountains is God's way of telling us that although it's not always easy to take the moral high ground, all who follow God's commandments are healed.

14

TIME OUT

A game of pretense
carries me through grief's drama
one scene at a time.

The Bible tells us to toil for six days and to rest on the seventh day. Most of us do an okay job following this rule, except when it comes to grief. Grief is hard work, yet we toil away night and day, week after week, month after month with no letup. Is it any wonder that so many of us feel exhausted and depressed?

We all need a break from work, from problems, and especially from grief. Give yourself permission to leave grief on the doorstep for an hour or a day. Take a day trip, go to a movie, or do something that requires your full attention.

Make a "safe" place in your house, and remove reminders of your loss, even photographs. Break away from grief as needed—not just on the seventh day but any time you need to catch your breath.

"God blessed the seventh day and made it holy . . ."

(Genesis 2:3)

"The Lord God took the man and put him in the Garden of Eden to work it and take care of it."

(Genesis 2:15)

15

GARDEN LESSONS

*Sunshine and shadows
depend upon each other
for their existence.*

Seasoned gardeners know the importance of preparing the soil before planting. A tree is more likely to withstand harsh wintry months if its roots are firmly established in good soil. Soon after I planted a bougainvillea, the weather turned cold, and I lost it. The plant wasn't strong enough to withstand a drop in temperature because the roots had not yet taken hold.

A lot of us "lose it" following the death of a loved one, and only a firmly rooted belief in God and the love of family and friends can keep us from toppling over.

Studies show that people with a strong relationship with God are healthier, are more emotionally mature, and experience less depression than nonbelievers. Those with a strong belief in God are also better able to handle stress, major illness, and the loss of a loved one. Soul work is as essential to our emotional and spiritual health as soil work is to plants.

Grieving is a time for personal repotting. By removing ourselves from the things that confine or prevent us from change, we make room for new opportunities that lie ahead. Lessons learned in grief can give us the courage to weed out negative people and trim away the dead wood in our lives.

After the death of her husband, a forty-four-year-old woman rid herself of the fears that were holding her back and landed the job of her dreams. "Having survived my husband's death, I now know I can survive anything, even rejection."

Grief is the time to nourish the roots of our faith and to nurture the people who add fragrant flowers to the gardens of our soul. Grief is the shade that protects us until we're strong enough to stand in the sunlight. Grief is the rain that helps us grow.

Repot a plant. Stand beneath the protective branches of a sprawling tree. Step into the sunlight. Leave a bouquet of flowers on someone's doorstep. Clean out your closets to make room for clothes that better reflect recent changes in you. Cross out the names of any negative people in your address book. If your faith has been uprooted, turn a listening soul toward God, and He will make His presence known to you.

Make room in your life for new growth, and you'll make room for your loved one's lasting gifts to flourish.

"The man who trusts in the LORD . . . will be like a tree planted by the water that sends out its roots by the stream."

(Jeremiah 17:7–8)

16

ATTITUDE ADJUSTMENT

*With each new sunrise
we're given the prospect of
a fresh beginning.*

How's your attitude lately?

A pilot can readily check the attitude indicator and know at a glance if the plane is leaning one way or another. The rest of us generally have to "crash land" before we give our attitude a thought.

The leading reason why students fail and people are fired from their jobs is poor attitude.

When God ordered the Israelites to "seek higher ground" and told Nicodemus that "ye must be born again," He was, in essence, saying "Hey, you need an attitude adjustment."

In his book *Attitude,* Charles Swindoll writes, "I am convinced that life is 10% what happens to me and 90% how I react to it."

Reaction is the key. Some people mumble and grumble over every little thing. Others manage to react in positive and life-affirming ways to even the most difficult trials.

We can grieve all we want, but nothing is going to bring our loved one back. A change in attitude, however, can help us find new meaning and purpose in life.

So how do we make an attitude adjustment? One way is to seek guidance from God. Belief in a Higher Being helps us put our lives in perspective. It makes us see the bigger picture. Another great way to change the way we think is to spend time with positive people.

If we choose to grieve and live our life on "higher ground," we keep the spirit of our loved one alive in the best possible way.

"Your attitude should be the same as that of Christ Jesus."
(Philippians 2:5)

Healing Ways

Putting a name to the emotions inside is an essential part of healing. Sometimes we don't heal because we're simply unaware of our own feelings.

We can't fix a problem until we know that a problem exists. That's why Psalms is a book made to order for the grieving heart. We see ourselves in David's lament: his shock, anger, and guilt resonate with us. His loneliness and fear are all too familiar. We understand his pleas, and suddenly we become aware of feelings that we didn't even know we felt. Our depression now has a name. What we mistook for anger might really be guilt. Confusion might really be fear. Identify your feelings, and then ask God's help in dealing with them. Feel the healing.

17

SPIRITUAL GROWTH THROUGH LOSS

With snail-like patience
I move out of the shadows
into the sunshine.

Some people never had anything bad happen to them, and yet they are warm, loving, and compassionate people. Other people seem shallow even though they've had terrible things happen in their lives.

You don't necessarily have to suffer to grow spiritually, but most of us are too caught up in our lives to take time out for inner reflection.

Then, wham! The unthinkable happens. We look our faith in the eye and find it lacking.

Grief changes the way we look at our work, and it suddenly seems meaningless.

Grief changes the prism through which we view the future, and we see only a bleak desert.

Grief casts a big shadow over relationships, making us feel emotionally and spiritually dead.

So what do we do when everything for which we've worked and in which we've invested our time no longer holds meaning?

First, acknowledge that questioning the purpose and meaning of life is a good thing. Robert Fulgrum wrote in *All I Learned About Life I Learned in Kindergarten*, "To be human is to keep rattling the bars of the cage of existence hollering, 'What's it for?'"

Rattle those bars by facing up to the doubts and confusion that you have about God. Pray for guidance and understanding. Seek counsel. Read and study.

Rattle the bars by asking honest questions about your job or career. Is it possible to find meaning in the work again? Or is it necessary to change jobs altogether? Are you willing to go back to school or take a cut in pay, if necessary? Perhaps the answer is to find more meaningful activities to do outside of work.

Rattle the bars by working on relationships. Reconnect physically with a spouse, partner, or other family members. Cuddle and hug—practice group hugs. Dance together, hold each other. Reconnect physically by playing and laughing together, by sharing. Keep rattling those bars.

"No mind has conceived what God has prepared for those who love him."

(1 Corinthians 2:9)

18

SPIRITUAL CRUTCHES

*Loving faith in God
leads us through the valley of
the shadow of death.*

A flamboyant governor made headlines by declaring religion a crutch for weak people. The controversy that followed puzzled me more than the statement. Why were people so up in arms, going so far as to call for his resignation? Is it because none of us likes to think of ourselves as weak? Or do we simply hate to admit that we need help at times?

The death of a loved one has brought some of the brightest, most creative, and most powerful men in the world to their knees.

Death makes weaklings of us all—so what if we need a crutch or two to get us through grief and despair? So what? No one would find fault if we used crutches after breaking a leg. So why shouldn't we avail ourselves of crutches if our spirit is broken?

So what if, in our grief, we hold on to God with both hands? No man can survive stormy seas for long without holding on to something.

Some people lose a loved one and turn to alcohol or drugs. These substances, too, are crutches, but they're crutches that deplete our inner strength, making it impossible to heal. Real strength, the kind needed to pick ourselves up no matter what life dishes out, comes from God.

So hold on to God with both hands. Wrap your heart around His compassion, your soul around His wisdom, your whole being around His love.

"God is our refuge and strength, an ever-present help in trouble."
(Psalm 46:1)

God Works Through Our Healing

[Jesus said], "But this happened so that the work of God might be displayed in his life."

(John 9:3)

John 9:1–12 tells the story of Jesus' healing a man who had been blind from birth. The man's neighbors were amazed and asked how he had been healed. When he told them that Jesus had healed him, the man opened his neighbors' eyes to God's work.

When God heals our grief, people notice. People ask how we got through it. How did we survive? This questioning gives us a wonderful opportunity to reveal to the world God's amazing healing powers.

19

SINS OF OMISSION

*The Great Creator
helps repair any problem
we allow Him to.*

When I had my first baby, I was told to lay him on his stomach as a precaution against Sudden Infant Death Syndrome (SIDS). According to my daughter, that's "old thinking." Today, young mothers are told to place babies on their backs.

Coffee is good for you; coffee is bad. The earth is flat; the earth is round. Scientific "facts" are proven wrong every day.

But are they really wrong?

Science writer K.C. Cole writes in her book *First You Build a Cloud* that scientific wrongs are really sins of omission. "They were wrong because they failed to take something into account, to see some part of nature that was keeping itself invisible, to notice connections among things that on the surface seemed totally unconnected. 'Wrong' more nearly means 'limited.'"

In times of grief, it's easy to think we were wrong about a sovereign God. How can an all-mighty, all-powerful God let children be murdered and people be tortured? How can He stand by while teens are gunned down in school? How could He let my loved one die?

But are we wrong? What have we not taken into account? What connections have we missed? What "sins of omission" are lacking in our faith?

Although we might never know the answers, it's important to keep struggling with the questions. The more we seek to understand, the more we realize the impossibility of our task. God is bigger than our minds can grasp. Everything you know or think you know about God is limited because no one, not even the smartest person in the world, has the mental acuity to understand the full scope of God.

> *"No one can comprehend what goes on under the sun.*
> *Despite all his efforts to search it out, man cannot discover its meaning."*
>
> *(Ecclesiastes 8:17)*

20

WHERE IS GOD?

Let God's light so shine
that it blinds the eyes of grief
and melts away pain.

The question was asked following the Oklahoma and World Trade Center horrors. We heard it following the Oregon and Colorado school shootings. A mother cried out the question upon learning that her daughter had been brutally murdered. It's a question that has been asked in the trenches of every battlefield in every war, a question that seared the souls in every Nazi concentration camp.

The question? *Where is God?*

Although it might not seem so at times, God is everywhere. We feel God's presence when a church prays with us. We feel God's love when a friend lends a compassionate ear.

We hear God's voice in a coworker's thoughtful words.

We internalize God's Word when we read from the Bible or listen to a sermon. We see God's face in the fireman who risks his life to save a child; in hospice workers; and in the minister, rabbi, or priest who counsels those on the edge of humanity. We recognize God when we act in love.

By letting God work through us, we can comfort a lonely heart or a grieving soul. We can turn seeds of doubt into trees of faith. We can plant hope in every heart we touch.

Where is God?

With His people.

"You will seek me and find me when you seek me with all your heart."
(Jeremiah 29:13)

One Step at a Time

God could have created the earth in minutes; instead, He created it over the course of several days. He could have wiped out the Israelites' enemies in a split second, but He did away with them little by little. God could create within us a perfect faith in the time it takes to blink an eye. Instead, it takes a lifetime for our faith to mature.

God does not hurry anything that has a profound impact on our future. God could heal us an instant, but to do so would only undermine the significance of our loss and devalue our pain. Instead, He takes us through each step slowly, lovingly. This is God's way.

21

CREATING A SAFETY NET

Grief is a high wire
stretching into the future
with no net below.

My husband and I like to discuss the Sunday sermon on the way home from church. One sermon on bad habits got me to thinking, and I asked my husband if I had any. Without the least hesitation, he replied, "No, and neither do I."

This pretty much sums up our marriage; he doesn't notice my bad habits, and I don't notice his. He doesn't notice when I over-spend, and I don't notice his extravagances. The list goes on and on, but it all comes down to this: each of us spreads a wide net for the other—a safety net.

Some brave souls go through life with no such safety net. When something goes wrong, they have no friends to believe in them, no faith to sustain them, nothing to break the fall.

We all need a safety net. We need friends whose approval we can count on. We need family members we can trust, and a close relationship to God. We need a faith that will carry us through the darkest days, a faith to hold on to in the darkest of nights.

We need a special someone who can share our most terrible pain, our most profound heartache, our deepest sorrow. A safety net should include a person or persons whom . . . we can call in the middle of the night—just to talk; . . . will cry and laugh with us; . . . sees our best even when our best isn't readily visible; and . . . allows us to grieve for as long and as hard as we want.

If you don't have a safety net, start piecing one together. Cultivate new friends, and reconnect with former friends. Join a place of worship or become more involved in the one to which you already belong. Work on your marriage or special partnership. Make God a priority in your life. Reach out to others, letting them know that they can depend on you. The next time you're tempted to criticize, sing words of praise instead.

Life is tough; don't try to navigate it without a safety net—the bigger, the better.

"If one falls down, his friend can help him up. But pity the man who falls and has no one to help him up!"

(Ecclesiastes 4:10)

Creating a Family Safety Net

Praying together at mealtimes strengthens each person individually and the family unit as a whole.

22

SECRETS

Spirits survive death
by passing wisdom and love
to those left behind.

My daughter loves her new role as a mother. "Why didn't anyone tell me how wonderful it is to have a child?" she asked me recently. "How could I live so long and not know this?"

How can you describe the wonders of motherhood? What words can possibly convey the joy and satisfaction of raising a child? And what about love? How do you explain falling in love? How do you describe the ecstasy of loving and being loved in return? Few words can adequately describe loneliness, joy, or even depression. There is no way to describe the loss of a loved one.

We can explain some of the pain and some of the heartache but only a very small part. Grief is a gradual unfolding of life's secrets. Secrets that surprise us. Secrets that horrify us. Secrets that make us shake our heads and wonder, How could I have lived so long and not know this? How could I not have known:

- how precious life is?
- how insignificant success is without someone with whom to share it?

- how shallow my faith was?
- how much time I wasted worrying about things that don't really count?
- that I filled my life with such meaningless tasks?
- who my real friends were?
- how strong and capable I am?

The loss of a loved one can be one of life's greatest teachers.

"The secret of the kingdom of God has been given to you."
(Mark 4:11)

"Jesus answered, . . . 'The miracles I do in my Father's name speak for me.'"

(John 10:25)

Are you feeling depressed, lonely, disheartened, and downtrodden?

Lucky you. According to Pastor Jeff Cheadle of the Simi Valley Presbyterian Church in California, you are a candidate for a miracle. Every miracle begins with a problem.

23

THE GIFT OF ANGER

When I hammer nails,
I pound some of the anger
out of my system.

With all of the pain and loss brought on by the death of a loved one, perhaps the most puzzling emotion that we face is anger. We don't want to be angry with the person we lost, but sometimes we can't help ourselves.

A friend of mine is angry with her mother for dying of lung cancer.

"Why didn't she love us enough to quit smoking?" she asks.

"I hate him for what he did to us," an anguished widow laments after her husband took his own life.

"Why didn't he take better care of himself?" a daughter asks after her father died of heart problems that he ignored.

Sometimes our anger is irrational. Why did he leave me?

Sometimes the anger runs rampant. It's not unusual for those who are in grief to feel anger toward doctors, society, God, and the church.

Some people believe that anger is a sin, but the Bible tells us that it's not what we *feel* but what we *do* with our feelings that determines whether anger is good or bad.

Anger is a gift from God, just as are love and joy. Anger can be a great motivator, an energizer, and a source of determination and purpose. Almost every successful war waged against human suffering and injustice began with anger.

It would be a far better world if more of us were angry about the right things. When someone is gunned down senselessly in school or on the streets, we *should* be angry, angry enough to bring about reform and change and angry enough to seek justice.

Today, get physical; admit that you're angry, and resolve to do something about it. Instead of swallowing your anger, ask yourself, How can I turn my anger into positive action that will glorify God?

"Be ye angry and sin not."

(Ephesians 4:26)

Healing Ways

So how do you get rid of the anger that prevents healing? First, ensure that it really is anger, and not just some other emotion dressed in angry attire. Hurt sometimes feels like anger. So do guilt and fear.

Once you know for certain that what you feel *is* anger, ask yourself the following questions. Is the anger helping or hindering my grief? How does it block the happy memories of my loved one? Is my anger worthy of the energy that it requires? Is my anger keeping me from healing? More importantly, is it keeping me from God?

If you answered *yes* to any of these questions, ask God's help to find more positive ways to work through your anger.

24

FORGIVENESS

*We must tear away
our Saran-like resentments
lest we suffocate.*

What does it mean to forgive?

Gerald L. Sittser lost his mother, wife, and a daughter in a car accident. Yet, in his book *A Grace Disguised,* he writes that he forgives the drunk driver who took away his loved ones. The thought that came to mind when I read this was *How could he?*

But then he went on to explain. "Forgiveness is more a process than an event, more a movement from the soul than an action on the surface, such as saying the words 'I forgive you.'"

As thought-provoking as this statement is, it's the author's next enlightening words that caught my attention: "I have no vain notions that I have finally and forever forgiven the one who was responsible for the accident. I may have to forgive many times more—such as at the weddings of my children and the births of my grandchildren . . ."

I never understood the notion of forgiveness. I'm not talking about small hurts or injustices done to me because those I readily forgive. I'm talking about major pain inflicted on me by people in my past.

My mistake was in thinking that I could forgive once and be done with it. Of course, that was never the way it worked. No matter how much I tried to forgive, something jarred a memory and I'd be back where I started from. I used to wonder what was wrong with me. Why can't I forgive?

Jesus tells us in Matthew 18:22 to forgive our brother "seventy times seven." If the pain is deep enough, we might have to forgive the same perpetuator for the same hurt many times over. A person who lost a loved one because of the careless act of another will have to forgive that person at every holiday, at every nonwedding or nonbirthday. At every family reunion. At every turn. It won't be easy, and it will require an enormous effort.

Today, forgive one person, even if it's only for a minute or a day. If you're not ready to forgive the big hurts, start with the little hurts.

Forgive the friend who said or did something insensitive. Forgive the family member who seemed distant and nonresponsive to your needs. Forgive the neighbor who seems oblivious to your pain. Forgive your loved one for whatever deeds were left undone. Forgive those people who have no way of understanding the depth of your grief.

Be prepared to forgive—seventy times seven.

"Forgive us our sins, for we also forgive everyone who sins against us."
(Luke 11:4)

25

BLESSINGS

The gift of giving
offers us greater rewards
than does receiving.

When my youngest son told us that he wanted to join the Marine Corps, we were, admittedly, disappointed; we wanted him to stay home and go to college. When our daughter's husband accepted an out-of-state job, we were heart-broken. Letting our children go has always been difficult for my husband and me, but no matter how much we worry or wish they would make other choices, they always have our blessings.

Bestowing blessings on another person is an oft-neglected act of love. When we give someone our blessing, we are saying, in essence, four extremely important things:

- You have my full acceptance and approval.
- You are highly valued and cherished as a person.
- Your potential and abilities are fully noted and appreciated, and I have great faith in your future.
- You have my support.

Many people live a lifetime without being "blessed" by another person. Many adults go through life trying to win a parent's approval. When the parent dies, they lose all hope of ever receiving the longed-for blessing, and this loss leads to depression and feelings of unworthiness.

My friend Lesley told me, "All my mother ever did was criticize me, even on her death bed."

Another friend, Josey, said, "I never could do anything to please my father. I'm still trying even though he's been dead for five years."

How can a person heal when so many past hurts remain unresolved?

Gary Smalley and John Trent, Ph.D., address this problem in their book *The Blessing:* "Some children will never, in this life, hear words of love or acceptance from their parents. . . . Some will try to break down the door to their parents' hearts to receive this missing blessing, but all too often their attempt fails. For whatever reason, they have to face the fact that their blessing will have to come from another source."

If we didn't receive the blessing from our parents, we must fill our lives with people who love and accept us and aren't afraid to tell us so.

Sometimes it helps to look into a parent's background. Knowing the circumstances of a parent's early life can help us understand why it was so difficult for him or her to show acceptance and love.

Consider the possibility that some people, even those who love deeply, simply can't show what's in the heart.

Finally, remember that the Bible says in Acts 30:25, "It is more blessed to give than receive." Bless the people in your life; tell them with a loving touch how much you care; tell them how much you value them with words of praise. Let them know with a smile and a reassuring pat that you're committed to them.

Blessing others is one way that we can feel blessed in return. It's another way of healing and being healed.

Blessings

"The blessing of the LORD brings wealth . . ."

(Proverbs 10:22)

Healing Ways

Making loss meaningful. This is perhaps our greatest challenge, but it's a necessary part of the healing process. How is it possible to find meaning in something that makes no sense to us?

Rabbi David Wolpe responds to this question as follows in his book *Making Loss Matter:* "When we change our lives because someone else has changed us or moved us, we create meaning for the other person's life."

We give meaning to our loved ones' lives each time we:

... listen to a friend   ... offer inspiration
... make someone laugh   ... say a kind word
... act out of love   ... lend a helping hand
... make God our priority   ... share God's word
... give thanks   ... spread hope
... praise God   ... show compassion

"I pray that you . . . may have power, together with all the saints, to grasp how wide and long and high and deep is the love of Christ."
(*Ephesians 3:17–18*)

26

LEGACY

The power of love
lives on beyond the people
who have shared its joy.

Accoding to an old proverb, we live as long as we're remembered.

A woman in her nineties recently confessed to me that the thing she most dreads about dying is that the memory of her dead child will die with her.

She worries needlessly. Following the death of her only child, this woman became a foster parent and provided a happy, safe home for countless children throughout the years. She will remain in her foster children's hearts for as long as they live and, as long as she is remembered, the spirit of her dead child will live on.

We can let the death of a loved one make us either hard or strong. We can let it fill us with either bitterness or compassion. We can allow it to either block out the world or, like the ninety-year-old woman, teach us to embrace it with open arms. We can let grief make us either the kind of person that others want to forget—or to remember.

". . .he who believes has everlasting life"

(John 6:47)

*Keeping traditions
allows past generations
to participate.*

27

COUNT YOUR BLESSINGS

*My nightly prayers
give me a chance to recount
my daily blessings.*

A young boy is shot at school, and his parents are devastated. A carload of teens goes over a mountainside, and a small town is stricken with grief. A young mother walks into her baby's room and finds her small son dead, a victim of SIDS. How is it possible to count blessings in the face of such tragedies?

In his book *Hostage Bound, Hostage Free*, missionary Benjamin Weir recounts the story of how he was kidnapped by Shiite Muslims and held captive for sixteen months in a small room. Manacled and blindfolded, he feared for his life. So what did he do? He counted his blessings. One by one, he made a mental note of all of the good things in his life. He had his health, faith, hope, prayer, and wife. He had a pillow, a blanket, a family, and a mattress. He managed to count thirty-three blessings in a single day and this helped him quiet his fears.

Counting blessings is the quickest way to restore balance in the face of disaster and tragedy.

If you think your world has ended and you have nothing for which to live, count the blessings of friends and family.

If you feel as though your heart is broken and your soul is shattered, count the blessings of health and soundness of mind

If you feel alone and abandoned, count the blessings of faith and prayer.

Counting blessings won't cure your grief, but it will help you heal.

"How great is your goodness . . ."

(Psalm 31:19)

28

THE GIFT OF GUILT

The windmill of guilt
drives my deepest emotions
to their highest pitch.

Sometimes the hardest part of grief is guilt. We obsess over what we did or didn't do, the missed opportunities to say *I love you*, the times we lashed out in anger or impatience.

A young woman can't forget telling her brother she hated him a week before he died in a boating accident. A mother is immobilized by guilt because of an argument she had with her son the day before he took his own life. A widower can't forgive himself for being away on business during his wife's fatal heart attack.

Guilt complicates and prolongs the grieving process by preventing the emotional and spiritual growth necessary for recovery. Self-condemnation and regret can all too often lead to depression or even suicide.

Guilt comes from goodness. Guilt is the conscience saying, "Hey, hold on. An inner moral code has been violated." Instead of beating ourselves up over real or imagined offenses, we can recognize the goodness that makes us wish we had done things differently or better, and work toward expressing our guilt in more productive and positive ways.

Guilt can tear us apart or inspire us to do great things. It can distant us from God or bring us closer to Him. It can imprison us in darkness or fill our world with light. It can be a lasting curse— or a lasting gift.

> *"Whenever our hearts condemn us . . . God is greater than our hearts, and He knows everything."*
>
> (John 3:20)

Heal My Guilt, Lord

So how can we escape the destructive forces of guilt when guilt is so much a part of our grief? We start by confessing our shortcomings to God and asking for His forgiveness.

Write down the things you wish you had done differently. Underline the goodness that can be found at the source of your guilt.

If you wish . . .

- you had been **kind**er, be kind to someone who least expects it.
- for another chance to say *I love you*, resolve never to let a day go by without telling the people in your life how much you care.
- you had been more **understanding** or **patient**, listen to a troubled adolescent or elderly person.
- you hadn't taken your loved one for granted, say a prayer of **gratitude** for all of the people in your life today.
- you could take back every un**loving** word you ever said, say something nice to everyone you meet.
- you had spent more **time** with your loved one, spend time with a shut-in, lonely relative, or child.
- you could resolve the mis**understanding**s at the time of your loved one's death, work on improving your relationships.
- for your loved one's **forgive**ness, resolve to forgive yourself.

*Years do not erase
our connection to loved ones,
they merely change it.*

29

OUT OF PAIN COMES THE GIFT OF A DEEPER FAITH

*I feel God's presence
on those special occasions
when I need support.*

Mom, it's time to update your computer. My son tells me this with surprising and irritating regularity. Once I get comfortable with something, I hate to change. Still, after my initial resistance, I'm always delighted to discover what the new software permits me to do.

Faith is a lot like modern technology. If we don't "update" it regularly, it's likely to "breakdown" when we need it most.

The confusion that comes out of grief can affect us spiritually. We don't know what to believe anymore. Sometimes faith falls apart because it's based on faulty assumptions.

So what do you do when your faith deserts you? When the God you thought you knew no longer exists? How do you go about updating faith? Updating your relationship with God?

One way is to borrow from late film critic Gene Siskel's favorite interview question: What do you know for sure? It was always fun to watch celebrities struggle with this question, but it's even more interesting to ask it of ourselves.

You can start by writing down all of the things that you know about your faith, all of the things that you believe about God. If you know only one *truth* about God, that's enough.

> *"For the word of the LORD is right and true;*
> *he is faithful in all he does."*
>
> (Psalm 33:4)

Where are you?" is the first question God asked in the Bible. He asked it of Adam in the Garden of Eden, but He also asks it of us. Where are you in your faith?

Those of us who are in grief might have a hard time answering this question, but we must answer it anyway. We must admit our failures, be honest about our struggles and doubts, and acknowledge our pain and confusion. God promises to help all who confess and ask for His help.

> *"Praise the LORD . . . who forgives all your sins and heals all your diseases . . ."*
>
> (Psalm 103:2)

30

SQUARE PEGS

*What a tangled web
our deceptions weave into
our cloak of mourning.*

We think we have it made. We think we know who we are and what we believe—then, wham! Something happens, and the pegs of faith and meaning no longer fit into their previous holes.

We don't know what to believe anymore. Trying to fit the loss of a loved one into former belief systems counts, in part, for much of the confusion of grief.

What do we do when we discover that the foundation of our faith has just crumbled beneath our feet, when faith and life turn in opposite directions?

Much of our belief system is steeped in tradition or conditioning. Our busy lives prevent reflection and study, so we let someone else do the work for us.

Religion can be so passive; the church tells us what to believe, how to interpret Scripture, and what words should come out of our mouth.

A faith that comforts and strengthens in difficult times must be our own. We can learn from the church, but only *we* can put faith into action. Scholars can interpret the Word and put it in its historical context, but only *we* can find hidden in the Scriptures God's personal message to us.

Faith, like grief, is an inner journey that requires full participation. If you're feeling at loose ends, do the work of your faith. Read, study, pray in your own words and join a small Bible study group. Worship and praise God in a way that is meaningful to you. Keep working until the pegs all fit in the right holes.

"Faith by itself, if it is not accompanied by action, is dead."
                                                              (James 2:17)

31

SIGNS OF HEALING

Death drops a curtain
on one act of life's drama,
but the play goes on.

On a recent auto trip, my husband and I were certain that we had missed the turnoff. We were just about to turn around when we saw a sign ahead pointing us in the right direction. Sighing in relief, we relaxed.

Searching for signs is part of every journey. Signs let us know that we're heading in the right direction.

Grief is a journey of the heart and soul. It's also a journey with an unknown destination. Most of us have no idea what lies beyond the dark tunnel. We know only that we must get through it. So for what kind of signs do we look? How do we know that we're about to travel into the sunlight again? Following are some of the signs of healing to look for on your journey.

Hope.   You begin to turn your attention outward. The future no longer scares you. You begin to make plans, set goals. Perhaps you decide to go back to school, take a trip, or make new friends. Grief no longer commands all of your attention. You begin to build a new life and invest time and energy into other outlets.

Change. You're no longer the same person, and you seek ways to change your life to better reflect the new, more authentic you. Sometimes this involves big changes such as a change in location or jobs. Sometimes change is reflected in little things such as a new hairdo or wardrobe.

Connecting. You feel less isolated and alone. You want to be with other people, to feel more connected. You feel closer to God, to family, and to your inner self.

Acceptance. You accept your loved one's death and are at peace with it. You can talk about it without doubling over in pain. You feel comforted by happy memories of the past.

Gratitude. You have a new appreciation for life and the people you hold dear.

Meaning. You know who you are and where you're going. You've found a new purpose in living, a new direction. You have made peace with God and mankind. You are ready to move into the next phase of your life.

"I am the LORD, who heals you."

(Exodus 15:26)

Follow the Star

We all have a star that we follow, a star that no one else can see. The star directs and guides us, even leads us. The star is the leading force of our lives, the source of our motivation and strength.

Sometimes we follow the wrong star, especially in our youth. We follow the one that is brightest or the glitziest. Then when a loved one dies, our star loses its luster or fades away in the darkness of night. This is especially true if our guiding star was based on material things. Money, power, or career can lose their hold over us the day a loved one dies.

John McConnell, founder of Earth Day, wrote, "For whatever reason, life remains a great mystery. But those who make the most of it are those who see a star, follow it, and respond to the wonder they find with respect and love in all they do. Here is a challenge to all who wish well for the future. Follow the star."

The only star that can keep us on course when things are the darkest is the star that is built on faith. When we make God the North Star of our lives, we might stumble and fall at times, but we will never lose the way.

Seasons come and go,
but God's love is like the sun,
constantly shining.

32

LOST INNOCENCE

Life's fragility
hides in our darkest closet
till death comes knocking.

Men generally see themselves as protectors. Women view themselves as caretakers. When our care and protection isn't enough to save a loved one, we are devastated.

We no longer have the confidence that we can protect or care for our family. We often react by becoming overprotective and suspicious. We have, in essence, lost our innocence.

With the loss of innocence comes the loss of trust. We tell ourselves that the world is a scary place. Love is scary. Better not take chances.

Rhoda claims that after her brother was killed in a traffic accident, she wasn't allowed to drive or even ride in a car not driven by her parents. Nine years after her husband died in a boating accident on their honeymoon, thirty-five-year-old Christine has yet to date again.

The loss of trust makes us focus on the negative; we think of only the bad things that could happen and act accordingly. Like a soldier on night watch, we are always on guard. We teach our children fear instead of love. We are so intent on preventing disaster, we literally block out the possibility of anything good happening.

Regaining trust takes time and patience. It means putting your faith to work and relinquishing control to God. It means putting the world in balance again and accepting that more good things happen than bad. It means letting go and taking chances.

The loss of innocence is often the root of gratitude. It's the knowledge that life is fragile and therefore more precious.

"Trust in the Lord with all your heart and lean not on your own understanding: in all your ways acknowledge him and he will make your paths straight."

(Proverbs 3:5–6)

33

A TIME TO GRIEVE

"There is a time for everything, and a season for every activity under heaven."

(Ecclesiastes 3:1–8)

A time to be born, and a time to die. It never seems like the right time for a loved one to die. Losing someone we love reminds us how short life is and how much we take others for granted. From the darkest ashes of grief is born a new appreciation for family and friends.

A time to plant, and a time to pluck up that which is planted. Every day we are given countless opportunities to plant seeds of friendship, seeds of faith, seeds of wisdom. Grief is the time to pluck up what we've planted and call up friends and faith to get us through the tough times. Grief is a time to plant new seeds of change, new seeds of hope.

A time to kill, and a time to heal. Sometimes it's necessary to kill off the part of us that wants to cling to the past. A normally dependent woman must learn to do for herself after her husband's death rather than transfer her dependency onto her children. Sometimes it's necessary to sever relationships that prevent healing.

A time to break down, and a time to build up. The loss of a loved one can make us question our faith, God, and His wisdom. Such questions demand that we break down our belief system and rebuild our faith on a stronger foundation.

A time to weep, and a time to laugh. It's interesting to note that the word *weep* precedes the word *laugh*. This order tells us that grief is not forever. We will laugh again, and even feel joy, but first and utmost, we must weep.

A Time to Heal the Heart
Ecclesiastes 3:4–5

A time to mourn, and a time to dance. To mourn means to share your grief with others. This sharing requires friends to listen and support you until such time as you are strong enough to return the favor. This giving and sharing is the true dance of friendship.

A time to cast away stones, and a time to gather stones together. So many of us harbor resentments and anger following the death of a loved one. It's not always easy to forgive or let go of the hurt, but it's a necessary step toward healing. Sometimes we don't even know why we're depressed or feel angry. This is the time to gather our stones—to put a name to the feelings inside—so that we can better deal with them.

A time to embrace, and a time to refrain from embracing. Grief is a time of discovery. We learn of what we're made. We need to keep ourselves open to new ideas and new interests. At the same time, we must be careful not to jump into new situations too quickly. Some people make the mistake of selling a house or remarrying before it's time to do so.

A Time to Heal the Soul
Ecclesiastes 3:6–8

A time to get and a time to lose. We naturally focus on our loss, but the time will come when we realize how much we still have and stand to gain in the future.

A time to keep, and a time to cast away. Many of us can't bear to part with a loved one's belongings. Sometimes we keep their room intact or their closet sealed like a shrine. This is okay for awhile, but the time must come when we let go of the past and look toward the future.

A time to rend and a time to sew. Grief can be a time to pull ourselves away from people or situations that keep us from healing, but it's also a time to repair broken relationships.

A time to keep silence and a time to speak. Grief is a time to pour out our feelings to others and to God. But it's also a time to listen. What is God trying to tell us?

A time to love, and a time to hate. We must devote ourselves to the task of grieving with the same devotion as newlyweds. Grieving is an act of love; the pain we feel is love that has no way of releasing itself. But there will come a time when we will want to rid ourselves of the darkness and depression and seek to find hope and joy in living again.

A time of war and a time of peace. We struggle with questions and doubts. We bombard ourselves with guilt. We fight for the right to grieve in a society that would rather that we return to our old self in three days. Emotions battle within us. But if we struggle and fight hard enough, we will finally come to accept a loved one's death and know peace. This is God's plan for us.

"A simple man believes anything, but a prudent man gives thought to his steps."

(Proverbs 14:15)

34

WHEN PART OF YOU
IS MISSING

Lilies spring from bulbs
to remind us how new life
valiantly blossoms.

A Vietnam veteran who lost a leg in that war regretted not being a "whole" father for his two sons. A Boy Scout leader who took his sons camping, fishing, and sailing, he devoted his life to his boys. He was a "whole" father in every sense of the word, but his self-image prevented his seeing that fact. He was handicapped not by the loss of his leg but by the way he saw himself.

Following the loss of a loved one, it's tempting to focus on the hole in our heart and to ignore the richness and fullness that still exist in our life. It's easier to dwell on our weaknesses than our strengths, to focus on our brokenness rather than our wholeness.

We can and must be whole again—even when the gaping hole inside feels like the Grand Canyon. Our surviving loved ones deserve no less from us.

So how do we function like a whole person when part of us is missing? We start by paying attention to those around us. None of us knows what the future might hold. Each moment, each day is precious and can never be replaced.

Each day we give in to our brokenness is one less day that we give to the people we care about.

Each day lived in the past is one less day to build a future.

Each day of despair is one less day of joy.

Each day consumed by anger is one less day to love.

"He who seeks good finds goodwill . . ."

(Proverbs 11:27)

35

THE ONLY "PERFECT" GIFT

*Kindness is a gift
you can share with anyone,
including yourself.*

Many of us have spent an inordinate amount of time in shopping malls and thumbing through catalogues looking for the perfect gift. We never find it, of course, and for good reason. The only perfect gift is the gift of self.

Because we know how precious life is, we are more generous with the time spent with family and friends.

Because we have struggled with our faith, we can now offer inspiration and guidance to others struggling with theirs.

Because we have pulled ourselves from the well of despair, we can now offer encouragement to the depressed.

Because we have refused to let loss make us bitter, we can now give the gift of positive thinking.

Because we have built a new life, we can now give the gift of hope.

Because of what we've been through, because of the pain of loss, we have more to give than ever before.

"A gift opens the way for the giver and ushers him into the presence of the great."

(*Proverbs 18:16*)

36

FROM GRIEF TO THANKSGIVING

Of all our blessings,
the ability to love
is God's greatest gift.

Prayer does not come easily during the early weeks of grief. To be effective, prayer demands focus and concentration, an open heart, and a quiet soul—and we have none of these things. Nor do we have the words. If finally the words do come, they are often angry or accusatory. "Why?" we might ask. "Why have you forsaken me?"

It's possible to chart our healing journey by prayer. When we stop asking God *why* and start asking *for strength and guidance*, we know that we're healing. When we stop praying with closed fists and start reaching out to heaven with open hands, we know that we're healing.

When we stop shouting God's name in anger and start singing it in praise, we know that we're healing. When our loss stops commanding all of our attention and our life becomes more God-centered, we know that we're healing.

When we stop bemoaning our loss and start giving prayers of gratitude, we know that we're healing.

"Be joyful in hope, patient in affliction, faithful in prayer."
(Romans 12:12)

All the people . . . when they heard Jesus' words, acknowledged that God's way was right . . ."

(Luke 7:29)

ABOUT THE AUTHOR

Margaret Brownley started her career writing inspirational nonfiction. She is a contributing editor of Bereavement magazine.

She is also the author of twenty-two novels written for Penquin, St. Martin's Press, and Time Warner and has written for television. Her books have been translated in fourteen languages, and her work has appeared in numerous anthologies. She is the founder of the Simi Valley Presbyterian Church Bereavement Care and Grief Center.

Haiku

Only seventeen syllables long and written in the present or future tense, the spirit of haiku affirms the positive themes found in *Grieving God's Way.*

About Diantha Ain: Haiku Poet

Actress, writer, poet, composer, artist, and teacher, Diantha Ain is a contributing haiku editor of *Bereavement* magazine, and her poetry and haiku have been published in many anthologies.

To order additional copies of

Have your credit card ready and call

Toll free: (877) 421-READ (7323)

or send $15.99* each plus $5.95 S&H** to

WinePress Publishing
PO Box 428
Enumclaw, WA 98022

or order online at: www.winepressbooks.com

*Washington residents, add 8.4% sales tax
**add $1.50 S&H for each additional book ordered